FOREWORD

by Terence Reese

It is a special pleasure to introduce a book by two old friends who stand right at the top of all that is best in the modern game. Kathie Wei's late husband, C.C. Wei, devised the Precision system — a sensible One Club system entirely free from the grotesqueries of most modern methods, and I am happy to say that the book he asked me to write, *Precision Bidding and Precision Play*, first published in 1972, is still a steady seller. Kathie has played the system with great success, winning four world gold medals.

Martin I have known for thirty years or more. In a way, he is unique in the bridge world. The majority of leading players form studious partnerships, many of which last for years. Martin has always been in the forefront of the tournament world, but you couldn't name his "partner": he will play a simple system with almost any good player and finish at the top of the field.

You will see in this book the effect of an exceptional talent. None of the deals are of the complicated sort that are commonly presented as problems; all have a subtle point and you will think, as you go along, "Good heavens! How much I've always missed at this game!"

CONTENTS

WHAT IS THE WORST THAT CAN HAPPEN?

Dealer East Game all

```
                    ♠ K10876
                    ♡ AK
                    ◊ J1086
                    ♣ 64
    ♠ —                          ♠ Q532
    ♡ J7632                      ♡ 10854
    ◊ K752                       ◊ 3
    ♣ J975                       ♣ KQ82
                    ♠ AJ94
                    ♡ Q9
                    ◊ AQ94
                    ♣ A103
```

West	North	East	South
		pass	1NT
pass	2♡ *	pass	2♠
pass	3NT	pass	4♠
pass	pass	pass	

*transfer.

This hand looks easy and certainly seemed so to the declarer. He won the club lead to avoid an untimely diamond through the AQ, then laid down the ♠ A, on which West discarded a heart. Not greatly perturbed, South played King and another spade, won by East. Declarer expected a diamond now, but East played King and another club, which was just as good.

After dummy had ruffed the position was:

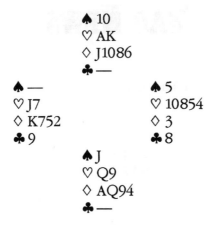

♠ 10
♥ AK
♦ J1086
♣ —

♠ —   ♠ 5
♥ J7   ♥ 10854
♦ K752   ♦ 3
♣ 9   ♣ 8

♠ J
♥ Q9
♦ AQ94
♣ —

South will lose two tricks now whether he leads a diamond or a trump from the table.

Kathie: That wasn't very bright play by the declarer, was it? It must be better to take the first trump finesse towards West. The only danger is a 4-0 break in spades, and if West has the long trumps it will be safe later to take the diamond finesse.

Martin: Yes, that's true. The line I was thinking of was to cross to dummy in hearts and lead the 10 of spades. If East follows you let it run, and if he shows out you can overtake and pick up the trumps without loss. An unusual way to play this trump combination, but it seems right here.

BAD NEWS

Dealer East Game all

```
            ♠ 842
            ♡ AQ
            ◇ AJ107
            ♣ J976
  ♡ 9 led

            ♠ K10
            ♡ KJ64
            ◇ K94
            ♣ A1082
```

West	North	East	South
			1♣
pass	1◇	pass	1NT
pass	3NT	pass	pass
pass			

It would not be very imaginative to rebid one heart on the South hand. No matter what the "system" may be, it is much better to conceal the tenace holdings in the majors.

West, as it happened, had a fairly obvious heart lead against 3NT. South won with the Ace and led the ♣ 9, on which the King appeared from East. South won and entered dummy with the ♡ Q to lead a second club. Bad news! East played the Queen now and shifted to a low spade. With little hope South played the king. At least the suit broke 4-4, so he was only one down.

This was the full hand:

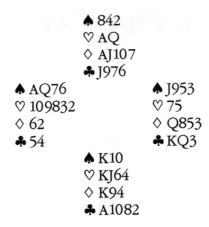

```
                    ♠ 842
                    ♡ AQ
                    ◊ AJ107
                    ♣ J976
   ♠ AQ76                        ♠ J953
   ♡ 109832                      ♡ 75
   ◊ 62                          ◊ Q853
   ♣ 54                          ♣ KQ3
                    ♠ K10
                    ♡ KJ64
                    ◊ K94
                    ♣ A1082
```

Kathie: South played on the wrong suit, of course. Spades was the danger suit, so he should play diamonds first, running the Jack towards West.

Martin: Yes, that's the right line, certainly. If the diamond finesse loses and West plays a cautious game, returning a heart, there will still be time to play for divided honors in clubs. The play is pretty easy if you think about it, but the declarer at a high level misplayed and lost the game.

— 3 —
A FINE TRY

Dealer South Love all

```
            ♠ AK
            ♡ AJ106
            ◇ 9762
            ♣ A108
  ♠ J led

            ♠ Q73
            ♡ KQ9875
            ◇ K3
            ♣ K4
```

West	North	East	South
			1♡
pass	2◇	pass	2♡
pass	6♡	pass	pass
pass			

North played a little game of his own in the bidding. The two diamond call, needless to say, was semi-psychic or perhaps just experimental.

South won the spade lead in dummy, drew trumps, and led a diamond to the king. West won and played a spade. The play took a long time now, but there was no miracle in the club suit and no squeeze, so the contract had to go one down.

```
                    ♠ AK
                    ♡ AJ106
                    ◊ 9762
                    ♣ A108
    ♠ J10962                    ♠ 854
    ♡ 4                         ♡ 32
    ◊ AJ5                       ◊ Q1084
    ♣ J753                      ♣ Q962
                    ♠ Q73
                    ♡ KQ9875
                    ◊ K3
                    ♣ K4
```

"Sorry, I didn't have much," said the South player. "Still, all we needed was the diamond Ace to be right."

Kathie: I don't see much in this hand, except that South ought to try for the drop of a doubleton ♣ QJ before leading the diamond from dummy; even if this is about a 100-1 chance.

Martin: There is another possibility. Suppose that South drops the ♠ 7 under the Ace at trick one, draws trumps, eliminates clubs, and plays the ♠ Q to the king. Then, when he leads a diamond to the king, it is quite possible that West, holding ◊ AJx and placing South with KQ10, may hold off.

Kathie: Yes, but if West pays attention to his partner's spade cards, he will not be fooled.

CHINESE PUZZLE

Dealer North Love all

```
                    ♠ AK98
                    ♡ 9
                    ◊ A53
                    ♣ KQ764
     ♠ J7632                      ♠ 1054
     ♡ J83                        ♡ A107
     ◊ 92                         ◊ QJ106
     ♣ A103                       ♣ 985
                    ♠ Q
                    ♡ KQ6542
                    ◊ K874
                    ♣ J2
```

West	North	East	South
	1♣	pass	1♡
pass	1♠	pass	2♡
pass	2NT	pass	4♡
pass	pass	pass	

Although many players would have taken more vigorous action with the South cards, the final contract was borderline. South might have preferred 3NT to four hearts.

When West led ◊ 9, South won with the King and planned to discard two diamonds on the top spades. The play continued: ♠ Q, ♣ 2 to West's ♣ A, ◊ 2 to ◊ A, two spades discarding diamonds, then ♡ 9 in this position:

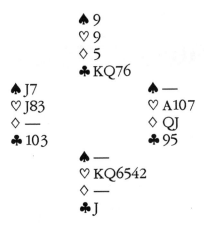

```
                    ♠ 9
                    ♡ 9
                    ◇ 5
                    ♣ KQ76
    ♠ J7                          ♠ —
    ♡ J83                         ♡ A107
    ◇ —                           ◇ QJ
    ♣ 103                         ♣ 95
                    ♠ —
                    ♡ KQ6542
                    ◇ —
                    ♣ J
```

The ♡ 9 went to the Queen and South returned a heart to East's 10. East tried a diamond, but South ruffed high and was home when all followed to the third round.

Kathie: With the hearts and clubs both 3-3, 3NT would have been easy, wouldn't it? Four hearts was a bit lucky.

Martin: Yes, it was, but look at the end position above. Suppose that on the ♡ 9 East plays the 10. South wins and returns a low one to West's 8. Now a fourth spade is ruffed by ♡ A and a third diamond promotes a sure trick for West's ♡ J. Difficult to see, even with all the cards exposed.

Kathie: Even on the line taken, West could have recovered by playing the ♡ J on the second round. Now the trump promotion can still be organized. A Chinese puzzle, you might say.

LOGICAL CONCLUSION

Dealer South E-W vulnerable

♠ K2
♡ 103
◇ Q8754
♣ KJ102

♠ 976
♡ AQ
◇ K62
♣ AQ987

South	West	North	East
1NT	pass	3NT	pass
pass	pass		

West began with the ♡ 4, East played the nine and declarer won with the Queen. A small diamond went to the Queen and Ace and the defenders continued with a heart. Declarer cashed his club winners hoping for a defensive slip-up. When nothing happened the contract was defeated.

This was the full deal:

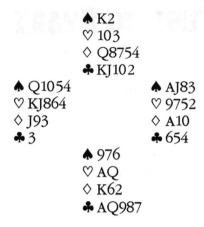

```
              ♠ K2
              ♡ 103
              ◇ Q8754
              ♣ KJ102
♠ Q1054              ♠ AJ83
♡ KJ864              ♡ 9752
◇ J93                ◇ A10
♣ 3                  ♣ 654
              ♠ 976
              ♡ AQ
              ◇ K62
              ♣ AQ987
```

South claimed that every card was wrong and besides East-West were cold for four hearts.

Kathie: That may well be so but it was difficult for East-West to compete as the bidding went.

Martin: Declarer's excuse seems rather lame to me. In order to succeed he needed to find one opponent with doubleton Ace of diamonds. As West is marked with KJ of hearts, if he also held the Ace of diamonds he surely could not hold the Ace of spades. He would then not find it difficult to shift to a spade. Therefore, the only logical play was to enter dummy and play a diamond to the King.

TIME TO START

Dealer South Love all

```
              ♠ 542
              ♡ 653
              ◊ QJ43
              ♣ AJ5
  ♠ AQ103              ♠ J86
  ♡ 102                ♡ KQJ9874
  ◊ 10985              ◊ —
  ♣ 743                ♣ 862
              ♠ K97
              ♡ A
              ◊ AK762
              ♣ KQ109
```

West	North	East	South
			1◊
pass	2◊	3♡	4♣
pass	5◊	pass	pass
pass			

West informed the table that his partner's 3♡ was a preempt— though what he would have done with an extra Ace is difficult to imagine.

West led the ♡ 10 to declarer's Ace. The play looked easy at first, but it became more difficult when East showed out on the Ace of trumps. The problem now was how to take care of the third likely loser in spades. Playing on reverse dummy lines, South led a club to the Jack and ruffed a heart with a low trump. He drew three rounds of trumps, then cashed a third club, arriving at this position with the lead in dummy:

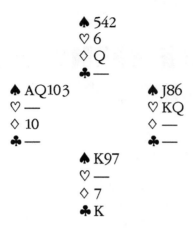

♠ 542
♡ 6
◊ Q
♣ —

♠ AQ103   ♠ J86
♡ —   ♡ KQ
◊ 10   ◊ —
♣ —   ♣ —

♠ K97
♡ —
◊ 7
♣ K

Dummy's third heart was ruffed by ◊ 7. It didn't suit West to overruff. Then declarer led the King of clubs; West ruffed and made only one more trick.

Kathie: I don't know how he did it. He began with three spade losers and lost only one of them.

Martin: The player who showed me the deal said that it occurred at rubber bridge and that the declarer was not even a tournament player.

Kathie: He'd better start soon!

WHEN TRUMPS ARE EMBARRASSING

Dealer North Game all

```
                    ♠ 652
                    ♡ J32
                    ◊ KJ4
                    ♣ A1063
        ♠ 109                   ♠ QJ874
        ♡ A1086                 ♡ Q
        ◊ A86                   ◊ 9752
        ♣ Q975                  ♣ J42
                    ♠ AK3
                    ♡ K9754
                    ◊ Q103
                    ♣ K8
```

West	North	East	South
	pass	pass	1♡
pass	2♣	pass	2NT
pass	3♡	pass	4♡
pass	pass	pass	

This was a somewhat old-fashioned auction, with both players bidding in aggressive style.

West's lead of the ♠ 10 ran to the ace. South entered dummy with the ◊ J and led a low heart, which was covered by the Queen, King and Ace. West led a second spade, which ran to the King.

South's only hope lay in some sort of trump endplay, or in causing West's second trump trick to coincide with declarer's spade loser. For the moment South played three rounds of clubs, ruffing in hand. When a diamond followed, West went up with the Ace and exited with a diamond to the king. Now South took another club ruff, which led to this ending:

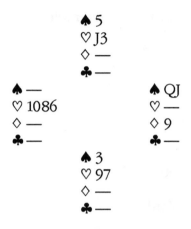

When a spade was led West had to ruff and concede the last two tricks.

Kathie: That was neatly done by the declarer, though I feel that West could have escaped the endplay.

Martin: Yes. When West is in with ♡ A, isn't it better for him to play Ace and another diamond at once? The difference is that since South doesn't have the chance to shorten himself twice in clubs, West can escape being endplayed in trumps.

TWO TRICKS FROM NOWHERE

Dealer East N-S vulnerable

$\spadesuit$ —
$\heartsuit$ AKJ75
$\diamondsuit$ KQ54
$\clubsuit$ AQ32

$\spadesuit$ J976
$\heartsuit$ —
$\diamondsuit$ J1097
$\clubsuit$ J10986

West	North	East	South
		pass	1$\spadesuit$
pass	2$\heartsuit$	pass	3$\heartsuit$
pass	4$\clubsuit$	pass	4$\diamondsuit$
pass	5$\diamondsuit$	pass	6NT
pass	7NT	pass	pass
pass			

Sitting West, you lead the $\clubsuit$ J, which runs to the King. South leads a low heart to the King, and for the moment, you can spare a club. The declarer follows with the $\heartsuit$ A from dummy, partner completing an echo, which you take to show strength rather than precise length. Meanwhile, what are you going to throw on this trick? All your cards look precious.

This was the situation, with West still to play:

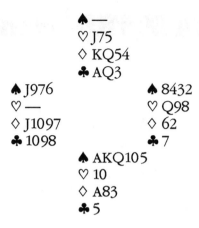

```
                    ♠ —
                    ♡ J75
                    ◊ KQ54
                    ♣ AQ3
    ♠ J976                      ♠ 8432
    ♡ —                        ♡ Q98
    ◊ J1097                    ◊ 62
    ♣ 1098                     ♣ 7
                    ♠ AKQ105
                    ♡ 10
                    ◊ A83
                    ♣ 5
```

At the table West threw a spade, which was disastrous. Can he do better?

Kathie: Usually it's right to unguard the suit held on your left, isn't it? Can't West let go a diamond safely?

Martin: Yes, he can. But the clubs also are held on your left. The reason why the diamond is better is that there is a control in this suit on either side of you. When the fourth diamond is played there will be no communication between the North and South hands.

ATTACK THE ENTRY

Dealer North Love all

```
                    ♠ Q102
                    ♡ A32
                    ◊ 32
                    ♣ K9642
        ♠ KJ64
        ♡ K654
        ◊ 75
        ♣ A105
```

North	East	South	West
pass	pass	1◊	Dbl
2♣	pass	3NT	pass
pass	pass		

West led the ♠ 4 which ran to declarer's nine. Declarer next played the Jack of clubs. West went up with his Ace and shifted to the ♡ 4. When dummy played small, East won the Queen and continued with the ♡ 10. West won declarer's Jack with his King and cleared the hearts. Declarer now played Ace, King, Queen, and another diamond. East won the fourth diamond and returned a spade.

This was the full deal:

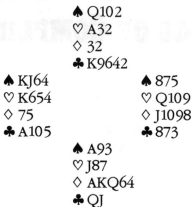

♠ Q102
♥ A32
♦ 32
♣ K9642

♠ KJ64
♥ K654
♦ 75
♣ A105

♠ 875
♥ Q109
♦ J1098
♣ 873

♠ A93
♥ J87
♦ AKQ64
♣ QJ

Declarer won the ♠ A, and this was the ending:

♠ Q
♥ —
♦ —
♣ K9

♠ K
♥ —
♦ —
♣ 105

immaterial

♠ 3
♥ —
♦ 6
♣ Q

When declarer cashed his last diamond, West was squeezed.

Kathie: When in with the ♦ J, East should stop to think. He should realize that playing a spade cannot help. He must return a club to break up the squeeze.

Martin: Absolutely right, it was smart of West to rise with his Ace of clubs at trick two. His attack on dummy's entry was the only reasonable chance for the defense.

25

EXCHANGE OF COMPLIMENTS

Dealer North Game all

♠ A86
♡ A105
◇ 32
♣ AJ975

♠ J led

♠ KQ2
♡ K642
◇ K764
♣ K8

West	North	East	South
	1♣	pass	1◇
pass	2♣	pass	3NT
pass	pass	pass	

So far as point count goes, North might have rebid 1NT, but in view of his lack of tenaces in the major suits he preferred two clubs.

West led the Jack of spades. South won with the King and played a simple game — King and another club. On the second round West dropped the Queen, and after consulting his ancestors, the declarer played low from dummy to prevent any possibility of East gaining the lead in clubs. This proved to be a clever trick, for the full hand was:

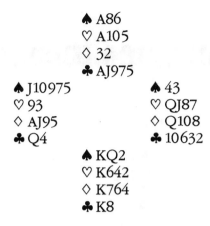

```
              ♠ A86
              ♡ A105
              ◇ 32
              ♣ AJ975
   ♠ J10975              ♠ 43
   ♡ 93                  ♡ QJ87
   ◇ AJ95               ◇ Q108
   ♣ Q4                  ♣ 10632
              ♠ KQ2
              ♡ K642
              ◇ K764
              ♣ K8
```

When West was in with the Queen of clubs he led a second spade and South had an easy nine tricks.

"Good thing you ducked the Queen of clubs," remarked North, as he entered the score. "We were wide open in diamonds."

"You were right not to rebid in notrumps," echoed his partner.

Kathie: Why were they so pleased with themselves? South could have played better, couldn't he? As the play went, it shouldn't have been difficult for West to drop the ♣ Q under the King.

Martin: True, and that's why South should have led clubs from the other side of the table — low to the 8. That is the best way to keep East out of the lead.

KANGAROO BIDDING

Dealer South N-S vulnerable

```
                ♠ AK10976
                ♡ AQJ10
                ◊ 876
                ♣ —
   ♠ 4                        ♠ QJ85
   ♡ K62                      ♡ 5
   ◊ J10                      ◊ 9532
   ♣ 9765432                  ♣ AQ108
                ♠ 32
                ♡ 98743
                ◊ AKQ4
                ♣ KJ
```

West	North	East	South
			1♡
pass	1♠	pass	2◊
pass	4♣	pass	4◊
pass	6♡	pass	pass
pass			

More than sixty years ago Ely Culbertson made the point that if on strong well-fitting hands the responder failed to make a forcing bid, he would lose time thereafter. It is strange that players are so stupid about this. Having responded one spade on this occasion, North had to jump around like a kangaroo. Still, the final contract was reasonable.

West began rather strangely with the ◊ J, and after winning this trick, South finessed ♡ 10 successfully. He came back to hand with a diamond and finessed the ♡ J, East discarding a club.

The position was now:

```
              ♠ AK10976
              ♡ AQ
              ◇ 8
              ♣ —
♠ 4                        ♠ QJ85
♡ K                        ♡ —
◇ —                        ◇ 95
♣ 9765432                  ♣ AQ10
              ♠ 32
              ♡ 987
              ◇ Q4
              ♣ KJ
```

   South drew the trump and played off ♠ AK but could do nothing when the spades broke 4-1.

Kathie: Declarer's timing was faulty. After taking the first heart finesse, he should cash the Ace of trumps and then play the ♠ A. He returns to hand with a diamond and plays a second spade. West can't gain by ruffing, so the King wins and a spade is ruffed. Declarer continues club ruff, spade ruff, club ruff and then discards his losing diamond on the good spades.

Martin: An interesting point about this deal is that if West begins with a club, declarer can easily make the contract by pitching a loser from the table at trick one, then finessing twice in trumps. Moreover, if by a miscalculation South lands in 7♡ , the contract can only be made on a club lead. After ruffing the opening club lead, South crosses twice to his hand in diamonds to take the trump finesse. He then cashes the trump Ace and comes back to the third diamond. Declarer now cashes his two good trumps. East is the victim of a triple squeeze and the grand is landed

AN INTERESTING IDEA

Dealer North E-W vulnerable

```
                    ♠ 54
                    ♡ AJ73
                    ◊ J54
                    ♣ Q762
        ♠ KQ7
        ♡ 82
        ◊ KQ62
        ♣ K965
```

West	North	East	South
	pass	pass	1♡
pass	2♡	pass	2NT
pass	4♡	pass	pass
pass			

This deal occurred several years ago in a European Championship match between Britain and France. The defense was made more difficult by the fact that South's 2NT was described simply as a game try, without reference to distribution.

The British West led the ♠ K against four hearts. South won, crossed to dummy with a trump, and led a low club from the table, East playing the 4 and declarer the jack. West won with the King. What should he play now?

It's a difficult decision. Willie Coyle, for Britain, returned a club, fatally for his side.

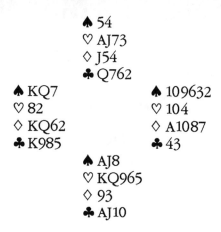

```
                    ♠ 54
                    ♡ AJ73
                    ◇ J54
                    ♣ Q762
    ♠ KQ7                      ♠ 109632
    ♡ 82                       ♡ 104
    ◇ KQ62                     ◇ A1087
    ♣ K985                     ♣ 43
                    ♠ AJ8
                    ♡ KQ965
                    ◇ 93
                    ♣ AJ10
```

Now the declarer was able in time to discard a diamond loser on the ♣ Q. He made ten tricks with five hearts, three clubs, ♠ A and a ruff.

Kathie: You can't draw any inference from a card played by a top expert as they usually falsecard. But you can glean information from the way an expert plays his cards. Here, declarer is marked with ♠ AJx. If he didn't fear a shift, he would have held up on the opening lead. The King of diamonds looks dangerous, but is probably right.

Martin: It was suggested in the French magazine that West might have led the ♠ Q when he was in. This gives East the chance to make a suit-preference signal. Holding the Ace of diamonds and nothing in clubs, he would have dropped the ♠ 10. An interesting idea, that.

THROUGH THE SIDE DOOR

Dealer West Love all

```
            ♠ KQ875
            ♡ AQ5
            ◇ A862
            ♣ 7

♣ K led

            ♠ AJ106
            ♡ 62
            ◇ Q943
            ♣ Q54
```

West	North	East	South
1♡	Dbl	pass	2♠
pass	4♠	pass	pass
pass			

West led the King of clubs and at trick two shifted to the Jack of hearts. He might have done this from a KJ holding, so South put in the Queen, which was headed by the King. East returned a heart to dummy's ace. South drew trumps, finding that West had a singleton and East three. Now he had to play the diamonds for just one loser.

He played Ace and another, hoping to find West with Kx, but this plan failed since the full hand was:

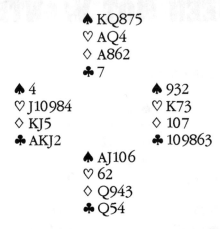

♠ KQ875
♥ AQ4
♦ A862
♣ 7

♠ 4
♥ J10984
♦ KJ5
♣ AKJ2

♠ 932
♥ K73
♦ 107
♣ 109863

♠ AJ106
♥ 62
♦ Q943
♣ Q54

Kathie: That trick of Gabriel Chagas would have worked well in diamonds, wouldn't it? What was it called? Yes, the intra-finesse. If declarer begins with a low diamond from dummy and puts in the 9, he can pin the 10 on the next round. This would have been a reasonable line after West had opened the bidding and shown up with a singleton spade.

Martin: Yes, and you don't need to find East with precisely 107 or J7. Any variety of Jx or 10x would do. Another point struck me about this combination. It is better play for East to insert the Jack from Jx or the 10 from 10x in this type of situation. This gives the declarer more chances to go wrong. For example, if the Jack (or 10) is played, South may be inclined to duck and play West for doubleton Kx, East for J10x.

— 14 —

QUEEN NOT WANTED

Dealer South Love all

```
              ♠ Q2
              ♡ J9754
              ◇ AK92
              ♣ Q3
 ♠ 983                  ♠ A1075
 ♡ 62                   ♡ 3
 ◇ Q5                   ◇ J1043
 ♣ J108742              ♣ K965
              ♠ KJ64
              ♡ AKQ108
              ◇ 876
              ♣ A
```

West	North	East	South
			1♡
pass	2◇	pass	2♠
pass	3♡	pass	4♣
pass	6♡	pass	pass
pass			

To the surprise of the audience watching on bridgerama, South covered the lead of the ♣ J with the Queen, which brought forth the King and Ace. The trumps fell in two rounds and a spade went to the Queen and Ace.

You can picture the position now:

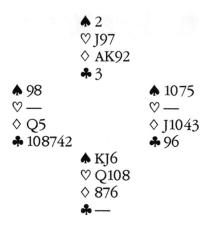

```
              ♠ 2
              ♡ J97
              ◊ AK92
              ♣ 3
    ♠ 98                    ♠ 1075
    ♡ —                     ♡ —
    ◊ Q5                    ◊ J1043
    ♣ 108742                ♣ 96
              ♠ KJ6
              ♡ Q108
              ◊ 876
              ♣ —
```

East, on lead, was happy to advance a club, but the sequel was disappointing for his side. South ruffed and continued with Queen and another heart. East discarded a club and a diamond, but the next heart was a killer. East parted with a spade, knowing his fate.

Kathie: That was neat play by the declarer. I can see that the Queen of clubs at trick one was unlikely to cost, because when the opponents come in with the Ace of spades they are likely to play a second club. Whether East could be blamed for not reading the position is not so easy to say. A spade back spoils the squeeze, does it not? Are you going to tell us who the players were?

Martin: No, it is more than my life is worth, East being a celebrated international. One point does occur to me: if South had been 4-5-2-2 he wouldn't have been worth four clubs over North's three hearts, would he? Remember, he had already reversed.

As Expected

Dealer South Game all

♠ A102
♡ A932
◇ A10
♣ AQ98

♠ K76
♡ K4
◇ KJ84
♣ KJ102

South	West	North	East
1◇	pass	1♡	pass
1NT	pass	6NT	pass
pass	pass		

West led the ♡ Q, declarer won in hand and cashed two rounds of clubs, East pitching a spade on the second. Declarer now played ◇ A and ran the ten.

This was the full deal:

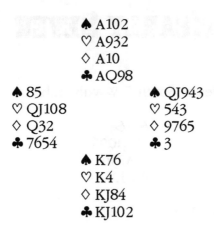

```
                    ♠ A102
                    ♡ A932
                    ◇ A10
                    ♣ AQ98
    ♠ 85                        ♠ QJ943
    ♡ QJ108                     ♡ 543
    ◇ Q32                       ◇ 9765
    ♣ 7654                      ♣ 3
                    ♠ K76
                    ♡ K4
                    ◇ KJ84
                    ♣ KJ102
```

The contract now failed. As expected the declarer claimed that he played the best percentage.

Kathie: Perhaps it is likely that East holds more diamonds. However, finding the ◇ Q with East does not solve the whole problem. It must be better to play West for Qx or Qxx.

Martin: I am sure you have noticed that 6♣ is virtually a lay-down, whereas 6NT is a gross overbid. Playing a natural system it must be right to open a club from the South hand.

NEARLY SEVEN

Dealer South E-W vulnerable

♠ A6
♡ Q1096
◇ AKJ6
♣ AK8

♣ Q led

♠ QJ
♡ AKJ875
◇ 742
♣ 62

West	North	East	South
			1♡
pass	3◇	pass	3♡
pass	4NT	pass	5◇
pass	5♠	pass	6♡
pass	pass	pass	

North's five spades was a reasonable move towards a grand slam. South had to sign off.

South won the club lead, drew trumps in two rounds, and cashed one high diamond. Then he eliminated the clubs and took a diamond finesse. No luck! East, who had begun with ◇ Q1082, won with the Queen and returned the 10. The last hope was the spade finesse, but this failed too.

```
              ♠ A6
              ♡ Q1096
              ◇ AKJ6
              ♣ AK8
   ♠ 10853              ♠ K9742
   ♡ 43                 ♡ 2
   ◇ 95                 ◇ Q1083
   ♣ QJ1075             ♣ 943
              ♠ QJ
              ♡ AKJ875
              ◇ 742
              ♣ 62
```

North was disappointed, but not critical. "Three things were wrong," he remarked. "Diamond finesse, diamond break, spade finesse."

Kathie: There's a better way to play the diamonds, isn't there, although it doesn't work here. The standard line for three tricks is AK, then lead towards the Jx, surely?

Martin: I believe you can do even better than that, because there is a finesse position in spades as well. Suppose you eliminate the clubs, then lead a low diamond. If West plays low you put in the 6, leaving East on play. If West goes in with the 9, you win with the king, return to hand, lead low again and cover West's card.

A low spade lead is more awkward for the declarer. He may finesse or he may go up with the ace, then eliminate the clubs and throw East in with the King.

A RATHER USELESS DUMMY

Dealer West N-S vulnerable

```
              ♠ 864
              ♡ 72
              ◇ 9862
              ♣ J763
♠ Q9532              ♠ KJ10
♡ 93                 ♡ 854
◇ KQ107              ◇ 4
♣ 54                 ♣ AKQ1098
              ♠ A7
              ♡ AKQJ106
              ◇ AJ53
              ♣ 2
```

West	North	East	South
pass	pass	1♣	4♡
pass	pass	pass	

East won the club lead with ♣ 10 and returned ◇ 4, which was covered by the 5. West won with the 10 and led his second club; South ruffed and drew four rounds of trumps, arriving at this position:

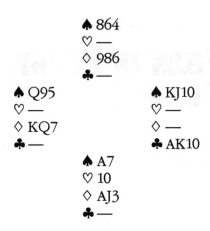

```
              ♠ 864
              ♡ —
              ◊ 986
              ♣ —
   ♠ Q95                    ♠ KJ10
   ♡ —                      ♡ —
   ◊ KQ7                    ◊ —
   ♣ —                      ♣ AK10
              ♠ A7
              ♡ 10
              ◊ AJ3
              ♣ —
```

    The declarer's play now was a low spade. East won with the 10 and led a club, which South ruffed. West, in a funny way, was squeezed on this trick. He could not afford a diamond, obviously, and if he throws a spade then South will cash the ♠ A and exit with a low diamond. One down was pretty good, considering the lie of the cards.

Kathie: It certainly was, since in looking at the diagram there seem to be five certain losers — three diamonds, a spade and a club. West can do better by giving his partner a diamond ruff, but to return a low diamond was risky.

Martin: There's another point, very easy to miss. Look at the position in the second diagram after East had won with ♠ 10. It seemed natural, or at any rate safe, to exit with a club, but this cost a trick as we saw. It is certain that declarer does not hold ♠ AQ, and a spade is better.

WHEN IN DOUBT, DRAW TRUMPS!

Dealer East Love all

```
                    ♠ 10642
                    ♡ AJ3
                    ◊ A764
                    ♣ A2
        ♠ J75                      ♠ —
        ♡ KQ109                    ♡ 87652
        ◊ Q1095                    ◊ J82
        ♣ KJ                       ♣ Q9643
                    ♠ AKQ98
                    3
                    ♡ 4
                    ◊ K3
                    ♣ 10875
```

West	North	East	South
		pass	1♠
pass	2◊	pass	2♠
pass	4♣	pass	4◊
pass	4♡	pass	5♠
pass	6♠	pass	pass
pass			

West's lead of the ♡ K was won in dummy, and the declarer played a round of trumps, expecting no problem. But when East showed out, discarding a heart, South had to reconsider.

At one table in a match the declarer could see no squeeze possibility, so he attempted to ruff two clubs in dummy. This plan was soon defeated.

The other declarer saw that to ruff two clubs successfully was well against the odds. He drew three rounds of trumps and followed with Ace and another club. West won this trick and had to risk the ◇ 10. South won, ruffed a club, ruffed a heart, and played the penultimate trump, arriving at this position:

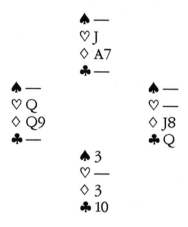

```
                    ♠ —
                    ♡ J
                    ◇ A7
                    ♣ —
      ♠ —                        ♠ —
      ♡ Q                        ♡ —
      ◇ Q9                       ◇ J8
      ♣ —                        ♣ Q
                    ♠ 3
                    ♡ —
                    ◇ 3
                    ♣ 10
```

Now the last trump won the money.

Kathie: That was well played by the declarer. I was wondering whether a diamond lead by West would have worked better. I find leading from KQ10 so often costs.

Martin: You mean because the opponents can lead a second diamond when they come in? Theoretically the declarer might ruff a third diamond and squeeze West in hearts and diamonds. The dummy still holds ♡AJ, remember.

THEY DISCARDED WELL

Dealer North Love all

<pre>
                    ♠ Q82
                    ♡ AK74
                    ◊ 8642
                    ♣ 86

        ◊ Q led

                    ♠ A73
                    ♡ —
                    ◊ AK
                    ♣ AKQ109752
</pre>

West	North	East	South
		pass	2♣
pass	2♡	pass	3♣
pass	3NT	pass	6♣
pass	pass	pass	

South's initial two clubs was conventional. When his partner showed values in hearts, then limited all-round strength, there was no sensible alternative to a direct six clubs. Partner might hold the right cards for seven, such as King of spades and Ace of hearts, but it wasn't going to be possible to find out.

On West's lead of the ◊ Q, East played the 3. South played off a large number of clubs, but the discarding was simple enough for East-West, as they could see that there would be no hope if South held any hearts at all.

This was the full hand:

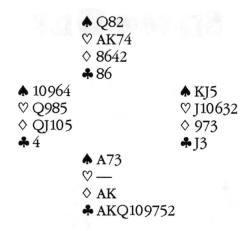

When the last club was played East came down to
♠ KJ5 and ◊ 9. It wasn't difficult for the defenders to take
two of the last four tricks.

Kathie: South was a bit innocent here!

Martin: He was, yes; and in case anyone hasn't noticed, all
he had to do after winning the first trick was lead
the ♣ 7 and overtake with the ♣ 8.

SELDOM WISE

Dealer South Game all

```
              ♠ KQJ2
              ♡ AQ5
              ◇ 1094
              ♣ AJ10
  ♠ 65                    ♠ 943
  ♡ KJ987                 ♡ —
  ◇ A82                   ◇ Q7653
  ♣ 754                   ♣ 98632
              ♠ A1087
              ♡ 106432
              ◇ KJ
              ♣ KQ
```

West	North	East	South
			1♡
pass	1♠	pass	2♠
pass	4♡	pass	pass
Dbl	Redbl	pass	pass
pass			

North's bidding looks a little quaint. Apparently he wanted to be sure that his side would be playing in a 5-3 heart fit rather than possibly a 4-3 spade fit. Most players would have doubled in West's position, but the usual result of such a double is that the opponents either transfer to a better contract or save a trick in the play.

Expecting to make at least three tricks in the trump suit, West began with the Ace of diamonds and followed with another diamond, which ran to the king. Warned by the double, South refrained from leading a trump. He cashed three clubs, ruffed a diamond, and played Ace and another spade to arrive at this position:

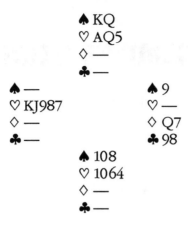

♠ KQ
♡ AQ5
◊ —
♣ —

♠ —
♡ KJ987
◊ —
♣ —

♠ 9
♡ —
◊ Q7
♣ 98

♠ 108
♡ 1064
◊ —
♣ —

West ruffed the next spade and exited with the ♡ J won by dummy's Queen. The fourth round of spades left West sadly on play. North-South registered 1080 (100 for a redoubled contract made, remember).

Kathie: Yes, of course it was silly to double. You always make at least one more trick on these hands if you don't double.

Martin: Most people know that — but they still double when they hold five good-looking trumps.

NO TIME TO THINK

Dealer South Love all

```
         ♠ Q2
         ♡ AQ9
         ◇ AQ102
         ♣ K1064
```

♣ 5 led

```
         ♠ AKJ10986
         ♡ 6
         ◇ 3
         ♣ QJ72
```

West	North	East	South
			4♠
pass	6♠	pass	pass
pass			

Obviously North should have bid 6NT in preference to six spades, but at two tables in a pairs event South became declarer and West led the 5 of clubs. One declarer put in the King of clubs from dummy and dropped the Jack from hand; the other played low and dropped the Queen under East's ace. Neither was "lucky", because East returned a club and West ruffed.

6NT by North would have been lay-down, as you see The interesting question is how South in six spades should have played to the first trick.

This was the full hand:

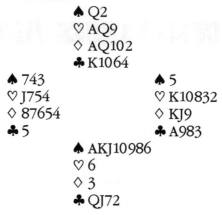

                    ♠ Q2
                    ♡ AQ9
                    ◊ AQ102
                    ♣ K1064
    ♠ 743   ♠ 5
    ♡ J754   ♡ K10832
    ◊ 87654   ◊ KJ9
    ♣ 5   ♣ A983
                    ♠ AKJ10986
                    ♡ 6
                    ◊ 3
                    ♣ QJ72

At the first table when the declarer put in the King and dropped the Jack under the Ace, it wasn't difficult for East to judge that couldn't have a stiff Jack (he would have played low from dummy). At the other table, where South played low from dummy and the Queen from hand, East reflected that West would not have chosen to lead low (third best, actually) from Jxxx.

Kathie: Each table got it half right. Declarer must show shortage in the club suit, and the only way to do that is to duck to the "stiff" Jack. Unfortunately, the play at each table gave East sufficient clues to determine that the only chance lay with a singleton club in his partner's hand.

Martin: Definitely, because no one leads from Jxxx against a slam (or for that matter rises with King holding a singleton Jack). You have to think quickly and play smoothly on these occasions. As a rule, you should aim to leave dummy with a tenace combination in the suit led.

— 22 —

CIRCUMSTANCES ALTER CASES

Dealer South Game all

♠ 32
♡ AKJ10
♢ Q3
♣ Q9754

♡ 9 led

♠ AK97
♡ Q64
♢ K72
♣ A103

West	North	East	South
			1NT
pass	2♣	pass	2♠
pass	3NT	pass	pass
pass			

South won the heart lead in dummy and tackled the clubs in a way that most textbooks would recommend — low to the 10. West won with the Jack and switched to a diamond. The Queen lost to the Ace and a diamond came back. South won the third round, crossed to dummy with a heart, and ran the 9 of clubs. Unluckily, West began with ♣ KJ6 and four diamonds, so the defense took three diamonds and two clubs. Not a good result for North-South, who held 28 points between them.

```
              ♠ 32
              ♡ AKJ10
              ◇ Q3
              ♣ Q9754
  ♠ Q8                    ♠ J10654
  ♡ 9872                  ♡ 53
  ◇ J864                  ◇ A1095
  ♣ KJ6                   ♣ 82
              ♠ AK97
              ♡ Q64
              ◇ K72
              ♣ A103
```

   "I could have made it if I had played the clubs differently," remarked the declarer.

Kathie: Indeed he could! It was wrong to take the first finesse towards West, was it not? A diamond switch from the East side is not so dangerous.

Martin: Yes, that's the main point of the deal. South has eight tricks on top, counting one in diamonds, so he must set about the clubs in the safest way. Suppose he begins with the ♣ 3 from hand and, at worst, the 9 loses to the Jack; then if a diamond from East runs to the Queen it will be perfectly safe to finesse the ♣ 10 on the next round. Leading the ♣ 3 from your hand is a perfect safety play.

TWO BAD BREAKS

Dealer South Game all

```
                    ♠ QJ96
                    ♡ K873
                    ◇ J752
                    ♣ 10
      ♠ 8432                    ♠ 5
      ♡ 10                      ♡ J965
      ◇ Q64                     ◇ K1083
      ♣ J9854                   ♣ Q763
                    ♠ AK107
                    ♡ AQ42
                    ◇ A9
                    ♣ AK2
```

West	North	East	South
			2♣
pass	2◇	pass	2NT
pass	3♣	pass	3♠
pass	5♠	pass	6♠
pass	pass	pass	

West chose to lead a trump and South won in hand. He played the ♣ A and ruffed a club, then took another round of trumps, discovering the 4-1 break. At this point there was only one trump in dummy, two in hand.

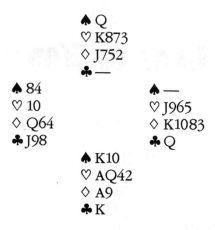

♠ Q
♡ K873
◇ J752
♣ —

♠ 84
♡ 10
◇ Q64
♣ J98

♠ —
♡ J965
◇ K1083
♣ Q

♠ K10
♡ AQ42
◇ A9
♣ K

South played off the King and ten of spades, discarding a heart from dummy. The second discard from the East hand wasn't easy, but eventually he did the right thing, discarding a diamond. Now the contract had to fail.

Kathie: Ruffing a club in dummy at an early stage doesn't look right. Isn't it better to aim for two diamond ruffs in hand? Begin with Ace and another diamond.

Martin: That's the way to start, no doubt. The defenders will play another round of trumps probably. After that you can manage only one diamond ruff, but you can then draw trumps and cash two clubs. East will be squeezed in hearts and diamonds at the finish. Oddly enough, a heart lead would always beat the contract.

LAND OF NOD

Dealer East Love all

```
            ♠ QJ105
            ♡ A10
            ◊ A654
            ♣ QJ8
  ♠ 962
  ♡ Q852
  ◊ K3
  ♣ A753
```

West	North	East	South
		pass	2♠
pass	4♠	pass	pass
pass			

In the 1979 World Championship match between the USA and Italy, the bidding was the same at both tables, and here West began with a trump. The Italian declarer, Franco, played two rounds of spades, on which East discarded low hearts, then led a club to the Jack and King.

It was all over now because the full hand was:

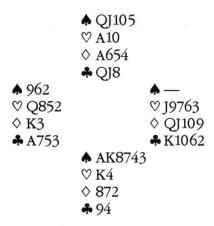

♠ QJ105
♥ A10
♦ A654
♣ QJ8

♠ 962   ♠ —
♥ Q852   ♥ J9763
♦ K3   ♦ QJ109
♣ A753   ♣ K1062

♠ AK8743
♥ K4
♦ 872
♣ 94

South ducked the diamond return, won the next diamond, and in due course discarded his third diamond on the Queen of clubs.

At the other table a heart was led against four spades and East played an even-numbered card, denoting weakness. South drew trumps, then led a club, and the play was the same as at the first table, South obtaining a discard on the Queen of clubs.

Kathie: Looking at the full hand it is easy to see that West should go in with the Ace of clubs and lead the King of diamonds. I just hope I might have done that at the table.

Martin: One must say that at this high level the defense should not have been too difficult to find. The Italian West was Pittala and the American West none other than Eddie Kantar. Oh well, the deal may be a slight consolation for those who have been defeated by his many brilliant problems in the American journals.

TRICKY TWO-SUITER

Dealer West N-S vulnerable

```
                    ♠ J72
                    ♡ J632
                    ◇ QJ54
                    ♣ A2
    ♠ 9                          ♠ Q1053
    ♡ AQ10974                    ♡ K8
    ◇ 1092                       ◇ AK876
    ♣ 983                        ♣ 54
                    ♠ AK864
                    ♡ 5
                    ◇ 3
                    ♣ KQJ107
                    6
```

West	North	East	South
2♡	pass	pass	Dbl
pass	3◇	pass	3♠
pass	4♠	pass	pass
pass			

This was the sort of hand that might be bid differently at each of ten tables. When two hearts comes round to him, should South call 3♣ or 4♣ or Double? As the bidding went here, should North have bid 2NT rather than 3◇ ? Well, we will just look at the play in four spades, noting only that East did well to pass throughout.

West led ◇ 10, which was covered by the Queen and King. East played King and another heart. South ruffed, cashed the ♠ A, crossed to the ♣ A, and led the ♠ J from dummy. East covered with the Queen and West showed out.

The position was now:

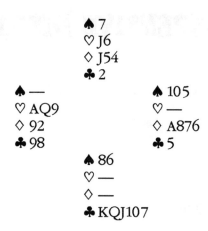

```
                ♠ 7
                ♡ J6
                ◇ J54
                ♣ 2
   ♠ —                      ♠ 105
   ♡ AQ9                    ♡ —
   ◇ 92                     ◇ A876
   ♣ 98                     ♣ 5
                ♠ 86
                ♡ —
                ◇ —
                ♣ KQJ107
```

All that South could do was play clubs and let East make his two trumps, for one down.

Kathie: In the diagram position South might have tried leading a club and ruffing with ♠ 7. If East is foolish enough to overruff...

Martin: Yes, I hadn't thought of that. What interested me was the early play after ruffing the second round of hearts. You are always going to make if the trumps are 3-2, so you have to think of the 4-1 breaks. I believe it's right to cross to the ♣ A and lead the ♠ J from the table. This is a mistake only if West has a singleton Queen. As the cards lie, you cover the Queen with the King, then ruff the third round of clubs with ♠ 7. East makes just one more trick whether he overruffs or not.

AN EXPENSIVE DISCARD

Dealer South N-S vulnerable

```
        ♠ 7432
        ♡ —
        ◇ AK765
        ♣ AJ97
```

♡ Q led

```
        ♠ KQ
        ♡ AK
        ◇ J43
        ♣ KQ10864
```

West	North	East	South
			1♣
Dbl	Redbl	1♡	2NT
pass	3♡	pass	4♣
pass	6♣	pass	pass
pass			

South discarded a spade from dummy on the heart lead and won in hand. He drew trumps in three rounds (West was void) and lost a spade to the ace. West returned a spade and in the end South's only hope was to bring down the Queen of diamonds in two rounds.

This attempt failed, for the full hand was:

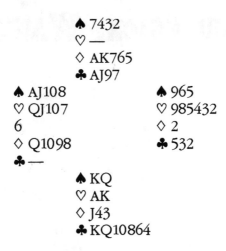

♠ 7432
♥ —
♦ AK765
♣ AJ97

♠ AJ108   ♠ 965
♥ QJ107   ♥ 985432
6   ♦ 2
♦ Q1098   ♣ 532
♣ —

♠ KQ
♥ AK
♦ J43
♣ KQ10864

South maintained that his partner, holding a useless void in hearts, should have proceeded more cautiously with four diamonds over four clubs.

Kathie: South should have thought about his own play and not criticized his partner's bidding. It was a mistake to discard North's long spade at trick one. If he throws a diamond and keeps the four spades, South can develop a squeeze in spades and diamonds.

Martin: Yes, that's right. After the third spade has been ruffed West will be in severe trouble when the long clubs are played out.

27

FOUR TRICKS WANTED

Dealer East E-W vulnerable

```
              ♠ Q98
              ♡ Q8
              ◊ QJ762
              ♣ Q95
                          ♠ KJ73
                          ♡ A54
        ♠ A led           ◊ AK
                          ♣ K1032
```

West	North	East	South
		1NT	2♡
pass	pass	pass	

In the days when par contests with prepared hands were more popular than they are now, producing good part score deals was always a problem. See what you make of this one.

West begins with the Ace of spades and follows with the ♠ 4, which you win with the Jack. The odds are strong that partner has led from Ax rather than Axx or Axxx. How do you plan the defense?

Most players continued with King and another spade.

This didn't achieve anything, because the full hand was:

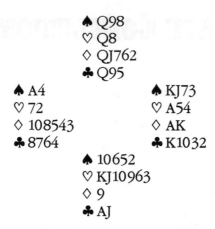

♠ Q98
♡ Q8
◊ QJ762
♣ Q95

♠ A4   ♠ KJ73
♡ 72   ♡ A54
◊ 108543   ◊ AK
♣ 8764   ♣ K1032

♠ 10652
♡ KJ10963
◊ 9
♣ AJ

After the defenders have taken the first three tricks they will make the two red aces, but that will be all. Looking at all four hands, can you see a better line for East-West?

Kathie: I have seen this hand somewhere, so I know the answer: East has to return a low spade at trick three; his partner ruffs and leads a trump. After Ace and another heart South loses altogether four tricks in spades and goes down one. It's a great problem.

Martin: Yes, and there's one tiny addition. At trick three East should return the ♠ 7, not the ♠ 3, just in case partner thinks of leading a club rather than a trump or a diamond.

28

SAFE CONCLUSION

Dealer South Game all

```
              ♠ 642
              ♡ 10643
              ◇ 953
              ♣ Q92
♠ KQJ10                  ♠ 953
♡ J95                    ♡ 872
◇ Q84                    ◇ K10
♣ 1074                   ♣ J8653
              ♠ A87
              ♡ AKQ
              ◇ AJ762
              ♣ AK
```

West	North	East	South
			2♣
pass	2◇	pass	3NT
pass	pass	pass	

West started the ♠ K and continued with the ten. South won the third round.

Prospects for the declarer aren't good; it looks as though he needs to find one of the defenders with the doubleton ◇KQ. All he could do for the moment was lead the ◇ 6, which ran to East's 10. Since the declarer was likely to hold the top cards in both hearts and clubs, East decided that the ♡ 8 would be as good as anything at this point.

After this trick the position was:

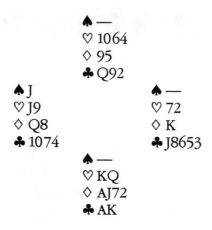

```
                    ♠ —
                    ♡ 1064
                    ◊ 95
                    ♣ Q92
        ♠ J                      ♠ —
        ♡ J9                     ♡ 72
        ◊ Q8                     ◊ K
        ♣ 1074                   ♣ J8653
                    ♠ —
                    ♡ KQ
                    ◊ AJ72
                    ♣ AK
```

South now exited with the 2 of diamonds. West tried
the Queen but East had to overtake and South made the
remainder.

"Well done," said North. "What made you read the
diamonds so well?"

Kathie: I think I can answer for South! If West had held Kx
          or Qx in diamonds he would have gone up with
          the honor in second hand. The only chance was to
          find East with the lone King at this point.

Martin: That's true, though not many players would have
          thought of it. Meanwhile, did you notice that East
          played poorly when he won the first diamond with
          the 10 instead of the King?

Kathie: As the play went, declarer had to rely on a mistake
          by the defense. On the actual layout, after winning
          the spade Ace, declarer should cash the Ace and
          King of clubs, Ace, King, Queen of hearts and then
          play Ace and a small diamond — the defense
          would rest.

29

FRENCH MUSTARD

Dealer West Game all

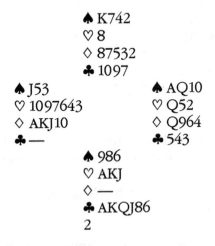

```
              ♠ K742
              ♡ 8
              ◊ 87532
              ♣ 1097
  ♠ J53                    ♠ AQ10
  ♡ 1097643                ♡ Q52
  ◊ AKJ10                  ◊ Q964
  ♣ —                      ♣ 543
              ♠ 986
              ♡ AKJ
              ◊ —
              ♣ AKQJ86
              2
```

West	North	West	South
pass	pass	pass	1♣
1♡	pass	pass	3♣
pass	4♣	pass	5♣
pass	pass	pass	

Playing at the Automobile Club in Paris twenty years ago, the French international, Roger Trezel, finished in five clubs. He ruffed the diamond lead with a high trump, and his first thought was that he might be able to establish a long diamond. It was a disappointment when West showed out on the first round of trumps. Continuing his play nevertheless, South ruffed a diamond, returned to dummy with a trump, and ruffed a third diamond Then he entered dummy with a ruff of the third heart and ruffed a fourth diamond, to which all followed.

These cards were left:

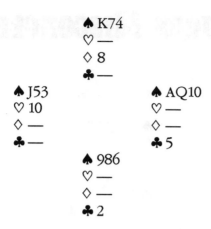

```
                 ♠ K74
                 ♡ —
                 ◊ 8
                 ♣ —
    ♠ J53                    ♠ AQ10
    ♡ 10                     ♡ —
    ◊ —                      ◊ —
    ♣ —                      ♣ 5
                 ♠ 986
                 ♡ —
                 ◊ —
                 ♣ 2
```

South had retained the 2 of clubs, you see. He exited with this card and after making a club and a spade East had to concede the last two tricks to the King of spades and the 8 of diamonds.

Kathie: Pretty as a picture! Most of us would see the winning play just a moment too late.

Martin: It's a deal worth remembering for that reason When it's easy to unblock, do so as a matter of habit.

30

A SERIOUS MISCONCEPTION

Dealer North Game all

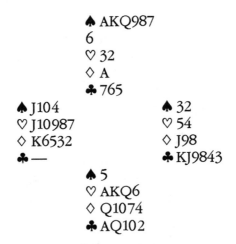

```
                  ♠ AKQ987
                  6
                  ♡ 32
                  ◇ A
                  ♣ 765
    ♠ J104                    ♠ 32
    ♡ J10987                  ♡ 54
    ◇ K6532                   ◇ J98
    ♣ —                       ♣ KJ9843
                  ♠ 5
                  ♡ AKQ6
                  ◇ Q1074
                  ♣ AQ102
```

West	North	East	South
	4◇	pass	4NT
pass	5♡	pass	6♠
Dbl	pass	pass	pass

This deal, famous in its day, was played during a Swiss pairs event at Miami about ten years ago. Amalya Kearse and Jacqui Mitchell were North-South against Canadians George Mittelman and Alan Graves, East-West.

North's four diamond opening signified a fairly strong four spades. Mitchell bid 4NT and advanced to six spades when she learned that her partner held two aces.

Why did Graves, West, double? Easy! He thought that North was declarer and he was making a Lightner double to attract a surprise lead — a club. When the bidding was reviewed it struck him that his double had been based on a serious misconception. Showing no emotion, he led a low diamond.

Mitchell won in dummy, came to hand with a heart, and advanced the 5 of spades, on which West played low. She finally concluded that West must have doubled on the strength of J10xxx in trumps and inserted dummy's 6! Realizing later what it was all about, she finessed the Queen of clubs, to end with thirteen tricks.

"If you had held the Jack or 10 of spades we would have got it one down," said West bravely to his partner. Mittelman's reply is not recorded.

Kathie: Yes, it was a wonderful story. As we aim to say something instructive about all the deals we describe, I wonder what you think, Martin, about these Lightner doubles when based on a void suit. In my experience they give away more tricks than they bring in.

Martin: I agree. Often they help declarer in the play, and sometimes they give him a chance to transfer to 6NT.

31

A TYPICAL
NINE-CARD PROBLEM

Dealer South Game all

♠ 9852
♡ KQ9
◇ K10864
♣ A

5♡ led

♠ J7
♡ A102
◇ AJ53
♣ KJ92

West	North	East	South
			1◇
pass	1♠	pass	1NT
pass	3NT	pass	pass
pass			

South won the heart lead in dummy and after some consideration played a diamond to the Ace and returned a diamond to the king.

West showed out, discarding a heart. When East came in on the third round he led a low spade. This proved a disaster for North-South, because West held ♠ A103 and the defense took four spade tricks to defeat the contract.

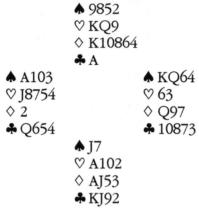

♠ 9852
♡ KQ9
◇ K10864
♣ A

♠ A103
♡ J8754
◇ 2
♣ Q654

♠ KQ64
♡ 63
◇ Q97
♣ 10873

♠ J7
♡ A102
◇ AJ53
♣ KJ92

"I played the diamonds like that in case West held all four," South remarked, as though he had done something clever. "If East holds four diamonds I can't pick them up."

Kathie: It wasn't at all likely that West would hold all the diamonds, was it? He was already marked with at least five hearts. Also, South should have thought about the danger of losing four spade tricks if the defenders gain the lead. It must be better to have West on lead.

Martin: That's right. West was much more likely to hold A10x, K10x, or Q10x of spades than all the diamonds. Apart from that, after West had shown length in hearts the odds distinctly favored East having longer diamonds than his partner. Thus there were two good reasons for beginning with the King of diamonds and finessing on the next round.

32

SIDE SUIT FIRST

Dealer East   E-W vulnerable

       ♠ K7
       ♡ J5
       ◊ QJ1087
       ♣ Q1063

♡ 3 led

       ♠ QJ1096
       5
       ♡ A
       ◊ 6542
       ♣ A2

West	North	East	South
		1♡	1♠
2♡	2♠	4♡	4♠
pass	pass	Dbl	pass
pass	pass		

North's two spades, with short trumps and what looked like good defensive values, was surely ill-judged, though it didn't do any damage on this occasion.

West led ♡ 3 and South played the Jack from dummy, a good play designed to give the impression that he held a doubleton. East covered with the King and South won. A low spade to the King was allowed to win and South returned a spade. Now the roof fell in, since the full hand was:

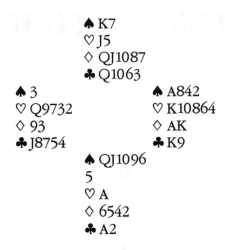

♠ K7
♡ J5
◇ QJ1087
♣ Q1063

♠ 3
♡ Q9732
◇ 93
♣ J8754

♠ A842
♡ K10864
◇ AK
♣ K9

♠ QJ1096
5
♡ A
◇ 6542
♣ A2

East captured the second spade and returned a heart. Now the defenders, holding two tricks in diamonds, were a tempo ahead. South finished an undignified two down.

Kathie: The second round of trumps was a mistake, wasn't it? East, for his double of four spades, was sure to hold ◇ AK, and it would have been wise to force out those cards while there was still a trump in dummy to protect against a forcing game

Martin: That's right; in fact, South might as well attack diamonds at trick two. They are almost sure to be breaking 2-2, because if West had held a low singleton he would doubtless have led it.

33

FORM A PICTURE

Dealer South Game all

```
            ♠ K10
            ♡ 8432
            ◊ J9864
            ♣ Q2
```

♡ A led

```
            ♠ AQ764
            ♡ —
            ◊ KQ107
            ♣ AK86
```

West	North	East	South
			1♠
Dbl	pass	2♡	3◊
3♡	5◊	pass	6◊
pass	pass	pass	

South had an obvious take-out double over East's two hearts, but he found a good home in diamonds. North's raise to five diamonds was well judged.

Rightly or wrongly, West began with the ♡A. South ruffed and led a low diamond, to which all followed. How should he continue, do you think?

At the table he led another round of diamonds, which wasn't quite good enough.

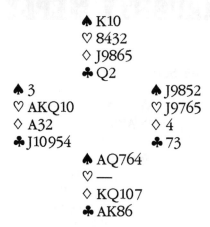

♠ K10
♡ 8432
◊ J9865
♣ Q2

♠ 3   ♠ J9852
♡ AKQ10   ♡ J9765
◊ A32   ◊ 4
♣ J10954   ♣ 73

♠ AQ764
♡ —
◊ KQ107
♣ AK86

West won the second round of trumps and led a third round. Now South had three losers — two spades and a club — and only two trumps in dummy. It was a mistake to lead the second round of diamonds. He should throw dummy's second spade on the third round of clubs and then crossruff, leaving Ax of trumps at large.

Kathie: Not many players would see that, though of course it wasn't difficult to work out West's distribution.

Martin: That's true. He was sure to have a singleton spade and also very likely to hold three trumps. I must say, I think it's a particularly instructive hand; it shows that you must know what's going on all the time.

— 34 —

HAUGHTY REPLY

Dealer South Love all

$\spadesuit$ 10964
$\heartsuit$ A85
$\diamondsuit$ 643
$\clubsuit$ K52

$\spadesuit$ J
$\heartsuit$ 92
$\diamondsuit$ AKQ10
2
$\clubsuit$ AQ976

$\diamondsuit$ 9 led

West	North	East	South
			1$\spadesuit$
pass	2$\spadesuit$	2NT	3$\spadesuit$
pass	pass	pass	

One of the oddities of the modern game is that there seems to be no fixed standard for East's 2NT in this type of sequence. Sometimes it is natural, usually based on a strong minor suit, sometimes it is a weak minor two-suiter and sometimes, as here, a fairly strong minor two-suiter. Occasions for a natural 2NT are rare, and our own view is that it is much more sensible to play the intervention as strong rather than a weak KJxxx and Q10xxxx type. When you are weak, and opponents have opened the bidding, the odds are that they will obtain the final contract. By intervening on a poor but shapely hand you simply assist them in both bidding and play.

On the present occasion West led $\diamondsuit$ 9 and East cashed three top diamonds, which wasn't clever because the full hand was:

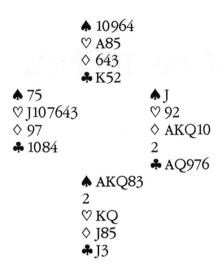

```
                    ♠ 10964
                    ♡ A85
                    ◊ 643
                    ♣ K52
        ♠ 75                    ♠ J
        ♡ J107643              ♡ 92
        ◊ 97                   ◊ AKQ10
        ♣ 1084                 2
                               ♣ AQ976
                    ♠ AKQ83
                    2
                    ♡ KQ
                    ◊ J85
                    ♣ J3
```

"Couldn't you have led a low diamond on the third round to make sure I could ruff and lead a club?" demanded West.

"I didn't think it would be necessary," replied East — who hadn't thought about it at all. South, of course, had dropped the Jack of diamonds on the second round.

Kathie: West was just as much to blame — he should have ruffed the third round of diamonds and shifted to a club.

Martin: I always find it amusing when the player who has made the worst mistake, in this case West, launches the first attack.

35

WAKE UP EARLY

Dealer South Love all

♠ 2
♡ K92
◇ KJ9754
♣ 1086

♡ 3 led

♠ AK1086
♡ AJ764
◇ —
♣ AK5

West	North	East	South
			1♠
pass	1NT	pass	3♡
pass	4♡	pass	6♡
pass	pass	pass	

West's lead of the ♡ 3 ran to the Queen and Ace. South played ♠ Ace and ruffed a spade, a club to the Ace and ruffed another spade, to which all followed. Now he ruffed a diamond and laid down the Ace of hearts.

He ended up one down, losing one trump and one club.

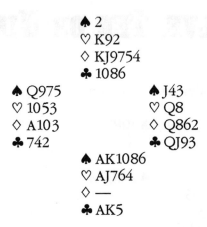

        ♠ 2
        ♡ K92
        ◇ KJ9754
        ♣ 1086

♠ Q975   ♠ J43
♡ 1053   ♡ Q8
◇ A103   ◇ Q862
♣ 742   ♣ QJ93

        ♠ AK1086
        ♡ AJ764
        ◇ —
        ♣ AK5

"Your hand wasn't much use to me," said South, who was unconscious of error.

"I think you make it if they lead anything but a trump," replied his partner.

Kathie: North was being tactful. Of course, South should go up with the ♡ K at trick one, as he intends to use the small trumps for ruffing. By the way, I'd be much happier to open with a conventional one club on the South hand.

Martin: As in Precision, you mean, your system. It's good for hands like this, I agree. One other small point: declarer should have tried a low diamond, or perhaps the jack, from dummy at an early stage. This may trick East, with a holding such as A10xx into going up with the ace.

36

TWELVE, TEN OR NINE?

Dealer East N-S vulnerable

```
                    ♠ 1087
                    ♡ A42
                    ◇ 2
                    ♣ AKQJ98
        ♠ J953                   ♠ 2
        ♡ 3                      ♡ KJ9765
        ◇ 986543                 ◇ AKJ
        ♣ 53                     ♣ 1042
                    ♠ AKQ64
                    ♡ Q108
                    ◇ Q107
                    ♣ 76
```

West	North	East	South
		1♡	1♠
pass	2♡	pass	2NT
pass	4♣	pass	4♠
pass	pass	pass	

This wasn't an easy hand to bid after South's one spade overcall. North managed it quite well with a cue bid in the enemy suit, then a jump in clubs. Wisely, as it turned out, he decided not to try for a slam.

West led the ♡ 3, and as this looked like a singleton South went up with the Ace in dummy. The declarer could see that twelve tricks would be laydown if the spades were breaking, but he decided that it would be safer, in four spades, to play a diamond. this would limit communications for the defending side, and so it turned out. East won the ◇K, cashed the ♡ K and gave his partner a ruff, but that was the end of the story.

Now suppose East, when in with ◊ K, had led a club. This leads to:

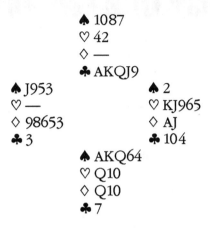

```
                    ♠ 1087
                    ♡ 42
                    ◊ —
                    ♣ AKQJ9
    ♠ J953                      ♠ 2
    ♡ —                         ♡ KJ965
    ◊ 98653                     ◊ AJ
    ♣ 3                         ♣ 104
                    ♠ AKQ64
                    ♡ Q10
                    ◊ Q10
                    ♣ 7
```

North, on lead, has lost only one trick, but can he make his contract now?

Kathie: I think so, there are several possible sequences.

Martin: Yes, there are. I've shown the position to one or two players who fancy their analysis, and none of them has found a way to do it against best defense.

Kathie: The winning line is a little double dummy. Win the club shift and continue with clubs. On the third club pitch a heart, West ruffs and can exit with a diamond or a trump. If a diamond, ruff in dummy, play a trump to hand and ruff your last diamond, then pitch your last heart on a club. If West exits with a trump, you have to win in hand, ruff a diamond and ruff a club high. Then ruff your last diamond and pitch your heart. Either way declarer loses only one diamond and two trumps.

37

JUST ONE CHANCE

Dealer North Love all

♠ K96
♡ K7632
◇ AK8
♣ 105

♠ 2 led

♠ 8
♡ A84
◇ 1052
♣ AKQJ98

West	North	East	South
	1♡	4♠	6♣
pass	pass	pass	

South was worth only five clubs over East's four spades, but he was the type of player who could not bear to be shut out. As he remarked later, fairly good hearts and the Ace of diamonds would have been enough.

West led the ♠ 2, won by the 10, and East returned a low spade. South ruffed and West discarded a diamond. Prospects seemed poor, because there were only ten tricks on top.

To find East with a singleton Jack or Queen of diamonds wouldn't help, but suppose East held a singleton nine. There would be chances if the full hand were:

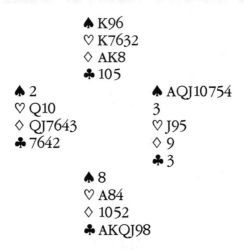

```
                    ♠ K96
                    ♡ K7632
                    ♢ AK8
                    ♣ 105
    ♠ 2                         ♠ AQJ10754
    ♡ Q10                       3
    ♢ QJ7643                    ♡ J95
    ♣ 7642                      ♢ 9
                               ♣ 3
                    ♠ 8
                    ♡ A84
                    ♢ 1052
                    ♣ AKQJ98
```

South mistimed the play, but the slam might have been made. After one round of trumps declarer must lead the ♢ 10, which West will probably cover, then run all the trumps. After a finesse of the ♢8 dummy is down to ♠ K, ♡ K7, ♢A, while South holds ♡A84 and ♢5. When the Ace of diamonds is led East has to retire.

Kathie: I suppose that sequence of play is logical, but I wouldn't entirely believe it.

Martin: Why not? A happy ending, anyway.

38

HE MUST HAVE SHAPE

Dealer South Love all

```
        ♠ Q102
        ♡ AK976
        ◊ 752
        ♣ 103
```

♠ 5 led

```
        ♠ A3
        ♡ 3
        ◊ AKQJ10
        9
        ♣ KQ96
```

West	North	East	South
			1◊
pass	1♡	1♠	2♣
pass	2◊	2♠	3♠
pass	5◊	pass	6◊
pass	pass	pass	

It wasn't an easy hand to bid. North might have tried 3NT over three spades, but he felt that this would not express his quite useful values. South was not altogether confident when he bid the slam.

The spade lead ran to the 10, Jack and Ace. South discarded a spade on the second heart, then led a low club to the King, which held. South continued a low club, which West won with the Jack. West exited with a low trump, on which East showed out. Then the ♣ 9 was ruffed, but the Ace did not fall, so South was one down. He couldn't ruff the fourth club because of West's ◊8.

```
                    ♠ Q102
                    ♡ AK976
                    ◊ 752
                    ♣ 103
    ♠ 54                        ♠ KJ9876
    ♡ 10854                     ♡ QJ2
    ◊ 8643                      ◊ —
    ♣ J72                       ♣ A854
                    ♠ A3
                    ♡ 3
                    ◊ AKQJ10
                    9
                    ♣ KQ96
```

Kathie: I suppose declarer could have made this if he had led the ♣ Q on the second round and brought down the Jack on the third round. Was that easy to judge?

Martin: If you think about East's voluntary two spades you must place him with good shape, because he is missing a lot of high cards. There is a good chance that he holds either ♣ Axxx or ♣ AJx. There are almost no situations where returning the low club after the King will help.

39

THE GIVE-AWAY

Dealer East E-W vulnerable

♠ J742
♡ AKJ84
◊ 106
♣ 92

♣ Q led

♠ AK1083
♡ Q5
◊ KJ3
♣ J87

West	North	East	South
		1♣	1♠
pass	3♣	pass	4♠
pass	pass	pass	

North's 3♣ was intended to convey that he had a sound, as opposed to pre-emptive, raise to three spades.

West began with the ♣ Q and followed with the ♣ 3. After the two tricks in clubs East played Ace and another diamond. South won with the King, cashed the ♠ A, then crossed to the ♡ A and led a second spade, on which East played low. After a little thought South finessed the 10, which held, and claimed the contract.

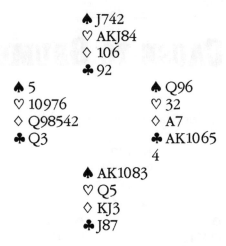

♠ J742
♡ AKJ84
◇ 106
♣ 92

♠ 5
♡ 10976
◇ Q98542
♣ Q3

♠ Q96
♡ 32
◇ A7
♣ AK1065
4

♠ AK1083
♡ Q5
◇ KJ3
♣ J87

"That was clever of you," exclaimed North when he saw his partner's cards. "You could place East with six clubs, yet you played him for three trumps!"

Kathie: It was a fairly well known situation, wasn't it? The fact that East didn't try a third club had to mean that he held the Queen of trumps and didn't want to give the show away.

Martin: East might have done a fraction better. Suppose he overtakes the ♣ Q and leads the ◇ A. Receiving only modest encouragement, he cashes a second club, then goes back to diamonds. This sequence might have distracted the declarer.

40

NO CAUSE TO GRUMBLE

Dealer South E-W vulnerable

```
              ♠ J102
              ♡ AJ763
              ◇ A2
              ♣ Q84
  ♠ 6                      ♠ 753
  ♡ K42                    ♡ Q1085
  ◇ 109864                 ◇ KQ7
  ♣ 9762                   ♣ K103
              ♠ AKQ98
              4
              ♡ 9
              ◇ J53
              ♣ AJ5
```

West	North	East	South
			1♠
pass	2♡	pass	3♠
pass	4◇	pass	4♠
pass	5♠	pass	6♠
pass	pass	pass	

West's lead of ◇10 was won by the Queen, and East returned a trump. South won in hand, crossed to the ♡ A and ruffed a heart. He then went to dummy's ♠ 10, ruffed another heart high and was now well placed, subject to the club finesse (sure to be right after that play at trick two).

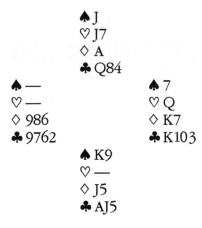

```
              ♠ J
              ♡ J7
              ◇ A
              ♣ Q84
  ♠ —                      ♠ 7
  ♡ —                      ♡ Q
  ◇ 986                    ◇ K7
  ♣ 9762                   ♣ K103
              ♠ K9
              ♡ —
              ◇ J5
              ♣ AJ5
```

The ♠ 9 went to the Jack and the fourth heart was ruffed by South's last trump. Now a diamond to the Ace and the fifth heart, squeezing East in diamonds and clubs.

"That was a lucky hand," remarked one of the defenders. "You had to find the hearts 4-3 and all the diamond and club honors in the East hand."

Kathie: There was something else, wasn't there? East must remove one of dummy's entries by returning a diamond to the Ace at trick two.

Martin: Quite so. If I were to venture a criticism it would be that there wasn't much point in the trump return.

Kathie: Strange. If trumps were 2-2 or if North had held ♠ J107 then declarer could succeed against any defense.

41

SUBSTITUTES ARE SELDOM LUCKY

Dealer North Game all

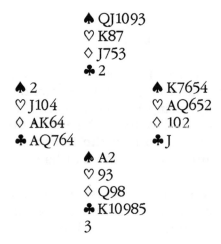

	♠ QJ1093		
	♡ K87		
	◊ J753		
	♣ 2		

♠ 2		♠ K7654
♡ J104		♡ AQ652
◊ AK64		◊ 102
♣ AQ764		♣ J

	♠ A2		
	♡ 93		
	◊ Q98		
	♣ K10985		
	3		

West	North	East	South
	pass	pass	3♣
pass	pass	Dbl	pass
pass	pass		

West began with the ◊ K and continued with Ace and another for his partner to ruff. What do you suppose that East played now?

Correct — the King of spades, to prevent any possibility of dummy gaining the lead to make anything of the ◊ J (East had ruffed with his only trump, remember). When South won with the Ace of spades and led a low spade, West ruffed. West then led the Jack of hearts and after two rounds of hearts the position was:

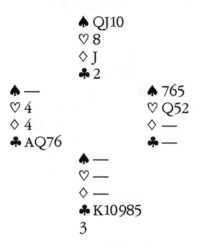

♠ QJ10
♡ 8
◊ J
♣ 2

♠ —   ♠ 765
♡ 4   ♡ Q52
◊ 4   ◊ —
♣ AQ76   ♣ —

♠ —
♡ —
◊ —
♣ K10985
3

Now East led a spade, South ruffed with ♣ 10 and West discarded, ensuring three more trump tricks for his side and a merry 1100.

Kathie: What a good defense! I have seen the hand before, but I don't know when.

Martin: It was a famous hand in its day. It occurred in a world pairs event at a time when I was just becoming interested in the tournament game. Alan Sontag was West and Peter Weichsel, East. Jim Becker, South, was playing as a substitute. Substitutes are rare in bridge, but the early morning — well, 11 a.m. — starts in some international events are a trial for competitors who normally are not alive at that hour.

42

TEST FOR COMPUTER

Dealer East N-S vulnerable

```
                    ♠ Q102
                    ♡ 2
                    ◊ AK9864
                    ♣ Q102
        ♠ AK3                    ♠ 4
        ♡ 854                    ♡ KQ1097
        ◊ 1073                   6
        ♣ 7643                   ◊ QJ2
                                 ♣ KJ8
                    ♠ J98765
                    ♡ AJ3
                    ◊ 5
                    ♣ A95
```

West	North	East	South
		1♡	1♠
1NT	3♡	Dbl	3♠
pass	4♠	pass	pass
Dbl	pass	pass	pass

North's 3♡ was intended to mean that he had a "value" raise to three spades. East's double was the pointless sort of call that simply gives the opposition more room to express themselves.

West did well to begin with Ace, King and another spade. South seems not to be well placed now; he can establish the diamonds but has no safe return to the table.

A very clever, and unusual, play saves the contract. Can you see what this is? South doesn't lead the Queen or Ten of clubs from the dummy, but the *Two!* Now East mustn't part with an honor because then South will establish the diamonds and enter dummy with a club. When East plays low South wins the 9, sets up the diamonds by ruffing the third round, then plays trumps to reach this end position:

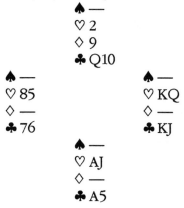

Now Ace and another heart is more than East can bear.

Kathie: I must say, that's a terrific play by the declarer. Funny that the low club from dummy leads to three club winners!

Martin: I agree. The hand shows how little we know about the game. I suppose a computer would find this line in a couple of seconds.

43

LOOK THE OTHER WAY

Dealer South N-S vulnerable

```
          ♠ AKQJ10
          9
          ♡ Q102
          ◇ A5
          ♣ 53
  ♠ 86
  ♡ J93
  ◇ QJ108
  ♣ K964
```

West	North	East	South
			1♣
pass	2♠	pass	2NT
pass	4NT	pass	6NT
pass	pass	pass	

North-South were playing a strong notrump, so South, on this bidding, was likely to have about 14-15 points. No suit having been agreed, North's 4NT was natural; at least, that was the partnership understanding.

Declarer won the diamond lead in dummy and finessed the ♣ Q. West won and played a second round of diamonds. This suited the declarer, since the full hand was:

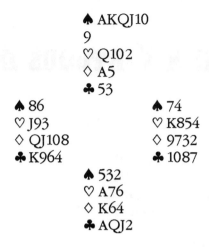

```
              ♠ AKQJ10
              9
              ♡ Q102
              ◇ A5
              ♣ 53
  ♠ 86                      ♠ 74
  ♡ J93                     ♡ K854
  ◇ QJ108                   ◇ 9732
  ♣ K964                    ♣ 1087
              ♠ 532
              ♡ A76
              ◇ K64
              ♣ AQJ2
```

West had turned up with honors in diamonds and clubs, so South decided to place East with the King of hearts. He crossed to dummy and led the Queen of hearts, forcing a cover. Then he ran off the spades, squeezing West in hearts and clubs.

Kathie: That was well done by the declarer, but no doubt it would have been better defense for West to look the other way when South finessed the Queen of clubs at trick two. If the club finesse is repeated the entries for a squeeze no longer exist.

Martin: That struck me too when I was first shown the hand. Players in 6NT who finesse a Queen at trick two always have AQJ. However, there's another interesting point: when ♣ Q holds it costs nothing to try a low heart from hand. If South takes the right view now, putting in the 10, he won't need the second finesse in clubs.

44

WITH A VIRTUOUS AIR

Dealer West N-S vulnerable

♠ K10
♡ J9754
◊ J109
♣ A75

♠ 7 led

♠ Q54
♡ AK
◊ AQ832
♣ K103

West	North	East	South
1♠	pass	pass	Dbl
pass	3♡	pass	3NT
pass	pass	pass	

When West led the ♠ 7 South put in the 10 from dummy, and East covered with the Jack. After a certain amount of calculation South played low from hand, but East led a second spade and the suit was cleared., South cashed the Ace of diamonds with no visible result and then the Ace of hearts. Again, nothing special happened. When South surrendered the lead the defenders took the King of diamonds and three more spades, a rather disappointing two down.

This was the full hand:

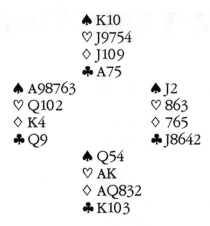

♠ K10
♡ J9754
◊ J109
♣ A75

♠ A98763   ♠ J2
♡ Q102   ♡ 863
◊ K4   ◊ 765
♣ Q9   ♣ J8642

♠ Q54
♡ AK
◊ AQ832
♣ K103

"That wasn't lucky," South observed. "I held off the Jack of spades because it might have been stiff. I tried the ◊A in the hope of a singleton King, and the ♡A because someone might have held a doubleton Q10."

Kathie: I won't wait for his partner to answer that, because the obvious game was to go up with dummy's ♠ K at trick one. It would be perfectly safe then to take the diamond finesse, with nine tricks guaranteed.

Martin: Do you know, I think the defenders missed a trick! If West had thought of dropping the 10 of hearts under the Ace South would have cashed the king. That would have been 300 down on a hand where North-South had a combined 27 points and a double stop in every suit.

— 45 —

DECLINE WITH THANKS

Dealer North Love all

```
              ♠ AKQ2
              ♡ AQ10
              ◇ AK
              ♣ QJ42
     ♠ J led
              ♠ 764
              ♡ KJ98
              ◇ J876
              ♣ A3
```

South	West	North	East
	pass	2♣	pass
2NT	pass	6NT	pass
pass	pass		

Counting two tricks in clubs, South has eleven on top and various chances for a twelfth. He made a good start, winning the spade lead in dummy, overtaking the ♡ 10 with the Jack, and leading a low club to the Queen.

This was the distribution:

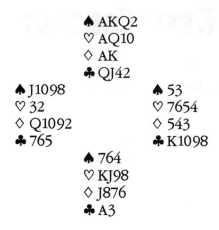

♠ AKQ2
♥ AQ10
♦ AK
♣ QJ42

♠ J1098   ♠ 53
♥ 32   ♥ 7654
♦ Q1092   ♦ 543
♣ 765   ♣ K1098

♠ 764
♥ KJ98
♦ J876
♣ A3

East headed the Queen of clubs with the King and returned the 10. Declarer cashed two diamonds and two spades, then played off the Jack of clubs and three more hearts, As you can see, this was very awkward for West, who was squeezed in spades and diamonds. Well played by South. Could the defense have done any better?

Kathie: It's more difficult for the declarer, isn't it, if East doesn't take the first club.

Martin: Yes, that's the point. Everyone knows that a declarer who is short a trick in a slam contract should normally seek to rectify the count by losing one trick early on. The game here was to stop him from doing this. If East doesn't capture the first club, then I don't think South can organize any sort of squeeze.

Kathie: Incidentally, I like the fact that North went directly to 6NT. To bid 3♣ over 2NT, looking for a 4-4 fit, is foolish. When you know you have the points for 6NT, bid it! Don't give the opponents a picture of your distribution.

46

KEEP CONTACT

Dealer East N-S vulnerable

♠ A2
♡ J83
◇ 10972
♣ AKJ5

◇ K led

♠ KJ9765
♡ A62
◇ A3
♣ Q4

West	North	East	South
		pass	1♠
pass	2♣	pass	2♠
pass	4♠	pass	pass
pass			

South won the diamond lead with the Ace, and did not ponder long before playing a spade to the Ace and a spade back. East showed out, discarding a heart. South won with the King and, still with fair confidence, played three rounds of clubs discarding his diamond loser. Clouds began to gather when West ruffed this, cashed the ♠ Q, and exited with a high diamond. There were still two losers in the South hand, so the contract went one down.

This was the full hand:

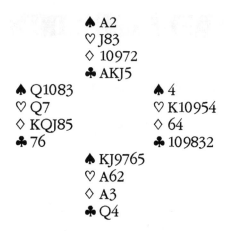

                      ♠ A2
                      ♡ J83
                      ◊ 10972
                      ♣ AKJ5

♠ Q1083   ♠ 4
♡ Q7   ♡ K10954
◊ KQJ85   ◊ 64
♣ 76   ♣ 109832

                      ♠ KJ9765
                      ♡ A62
                      ◊ A3
                      ♣ Q4

"Did you see that?" exclaimed the declarer. "The spades had to break 4-1 on the wrong side and the clubs had to be 5-2."

Kathie: After ♠ AK had revealed the 4-1 break it might have been a good idea to play a third round, discarding a diamond from dummy. This might tempt West to play Queen and Jack of diamonds instead of switching to hearts; then South can knock out the trump and discard his heart losers on the long clubs. But South was wrong earlier to cut himself off from dummy by playing the Ace and another spade.

Martin: Yes, that's the real point. South's best line is to cash the King of spades, then play three rounds of clubs. The defenders may ruff, but the ♠ A will still be an entry for the fourth club.

47

Two Fine Lines

Dealer South Love all

```
                    ♠ A10975
                    4
                    ♡ 9852
                    ◊ A109
                    ♣ —
      ♠ KQ                         ♠ J8632
      ♡ K10764                     ♡ Q3
      ◊ 4                          ◊ 632
      ♣ KQ986                      ♣ 743
                    ♠ —
                    ♡ AJ
                    ◊ KQJ875
                    ♣ AJ1052
```

West	North	East	South
			1◊
2NT	3♠	pass	5◊
pass	6◊	pass	pass
pass			

West's 2NT was part of the Michaels convention. It indicated a two-suiter in the other minor and the suit immediately above, hearts; therefore, South had no reason to mention his club suit.

West began with his singleton trump, as it was certain that the dummy hand expected to do some ruffing. South discarded his heart loser on the ♠ A and ruffed a spade bringing down West's ♠ KQ. He continued with a spade-club crossruff and a second trump, reaching this position:

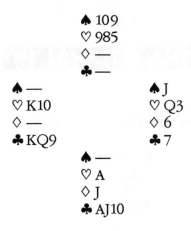

♠ 109
♥ 985
♦ —
♣ —

♠ —
♥ K10
♦ —
♣ KQ9

♠ J
♥ Q3
♦ 6
♣ 7

♠ —
♥ A
♦ J
♣ AJ10

On the last trump West had to throw a heart. Then South cashed the Ace of hearts and exited with the ♣J to make the last two tricks.

Kathie: That was very well played; note that South had to retain the ♥A for the endgame.

Martin: I agree, but I was thinking of a different line. After ♠A and a spade ruff, declarer can be certain that West's shape is 2-5-1-5. Then he can set up a twelfth trick by running the ♠10 through East and making a trick later with the 9. This line wins irrespective of West's precise holding in clubs.

Kathie: I'm not very keen myself on these two-suited overcalls. They achieve little and give a lot away.

48

A GIFT DECLINED

Dealer South N-S vulnerable

```
        ♠ AJ1087
        ♡ 32
        ◇ A6
        ♣ 10932
```

◇ K led

```
        ♠ K52
        ♡ KQ109876
        ◇ 2
        ♣ 54
```

West	North	East	South
			3♡
Dbl	pass	pass	pass

Declarer won with the Ace of diamonds in dummy and played a trump to his 9 (already gaining one trick from East's penalty pass). A spade to the 10 followed, then a second heart from dummy. East put up the Ace and led the ♣ 7, which was won by West's Jack. Now the second round of spades was ruffed by East, a low club gave West the lead, and another spade ruff defeated the contract. South's early joy was dispersed. Could he have helped it?

This was the full hand:

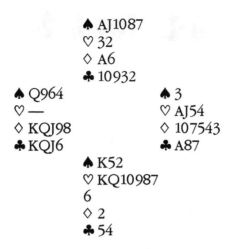

```
                    ♠ AJ1087
                    ♡ 32
                    ◊ A6
                    ♣ 10932
    ♠ Q964                      ♠ 3
    ♡ —                         ♡ AJ54
    ◊ KQJ98                     ◊ 107543
    ♣ KQJ6                      ♣ A87
                    ♠ K52
                    ♡ KQ10987
                    6
                    ◊ 2
                    ♣ 54
```

The result was particularly unfortunate for East-West because five diamonds was lay-down for them.

Kathie: Before I look at the play, East's pass of three hearts doubled was certainly questionable. It just pin-pointed the trump distribution. His partner was sure to have length in the minors, so five diamonds would have been reasonably safe. As for the play, South can afford to lose two hearts and two clubs, so the only way he could go down was by walking into two ruffs.

Martin: Quite so. The funny thing is that at the table nobody seemed to see this rather simple point.

Kathie: When the ♡ 9 wins, declarer should continue with a small club attempting to cut the opponents' communication.

49

4-1, NOT 3-2

Dealer East N-S vulnerable

♠ AJ9
♡ K763
◊ Q
♣ KJ742

♠ K led

♠ 874
♡ AJ985
◊ AJ
♣ A85

West	North	East	South
		3◊	3♡
pass	4NT	pass	5♣
pass	6♡	pass	pass
pass			

As quite often happens, the pre-emptive bid by East had the result of promoting his opponents into a slam they might not otherwise have reached. South's five clubs, in response to 4NT, showed 0 or 3 aces.

West led the ♠ K, won by dummy's Ace, and two rounds of hearts left West with the Queen. South played a club to the ace, East dropping the nine. A finesse of the Jack won the next trick, but when East showed out, it was impossible to avoid a spade loser.

This was the full hand:

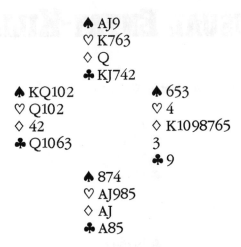

```
                    ♠ AJ9
                    ♡ K763
                    ◇ Q
                    ♣ KJ742
    ♠ KQ102                     ♠ 653
    ♡ Q102                      ♡ 4
    ◇ 42                        ◇ K1098765
    ♣ Q1063                     3
                                ♣ 9
                    ♠ 874
                    ♡ AJ985
                    ◇ AJ
                    ♣ A85
```

"My hand wasn't strong," South admitted. "I was tempted to tell a lie and indicate only two aces over 4NT."

Kathie: I haven't worked it out, but I should imagine that South ought to have played the clubs differently. If he had found them 3-2 he would have been able to dispose of only one spade before West ruffed.

Martin: Yes, that's the point. When the ♣9 fell from East the best chance — the only chance — was to play him for a singleton. Play the ♣8 and run it if not covered. If it is covered by the 10, finesse the Jack, return to the ◇A and pick up two more club tricks to dispose of your spade losers.

50

UNUSUAL ENTRY-KILLER

Dealer East E-W vulnerable

> ♠ AK5
> ♡ 1032
> ◇ 1076
> ♣ J1032

♡ 5 led

> ♠ J97642
> ♡ K4
> ◇ AK8
> ♣ A4

When East opened one heart South might have doubled, bid one spade or (if playing strong jump overcalls) two spades. He chose one spade and the bidding continued:

South	West	North	East
			1♡
1♠	pass	2♠	pass
4♠	pass	pass	pass

Following the modern fashion, West led low from three small. East won the Ace and returned the ◇ Q. South won the Ace and cashed two top trumps, which left West with the Queen. The only remaining chance was to drop a doubleton QJ of diamonds. When this plan failed, South was one down.

This was the full hand:

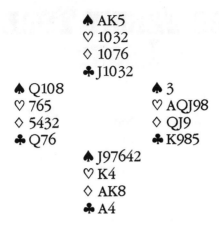

```
                    ♠ AK5
                    ♡ 1032
                    ◊ 1076
                    ♣ J1032
   ♠ Q108                        ♠ 3
   ♡ 765                         ♡ AQJ98
   ◊ 5432                        ◊ QJ9
   ♣ Q76                         ♣ K985
                    ♠ J97642
                    ♡ K4
                    ◊ AK8
                    ♣ A4
```

Kathie: I agree with the one spade overcall in preference to a double. As for the play, South might have given the clubs a run. There are several chances for an extra trick there.

Martin: Yes, that's right; including the way they lay here. If South plays Ace and another club as soon as he is in, he can develop an extra trick by bringing down the Queen on the third round. And there's another interesting point: if East, after winning the first trick with the ♡ A, returns a trump, he kills an important entry to the table. Not at all easy, I agree.

51

MORE TRICKY THAN IT LOOKS

Dealer South N-S vulnerable

```
                ♠ AQ108
                ♡ QJ1097
                ◇ Q2
                ♣ 54
                        ♠ 765
                        ♡ A42
        ♡ 6 led          ◇ 10986
                        ♣ K87
```

West	North	East	South
			1NT
pass	2◇	pass	2♡
pass	2♠	pass	4♡
pass	pass	pass	

South's 1NT was 15-17. North's 2◇ was a transfer and 2♠ (though there are other uses for this sequence) was natural.

West's lead of the six of hearts ran to the Ace. It didn't seem clear to East whether he should return a diamond or a club at this point; and if a club, which club? In the end he led the ♣ 7.

This turned out to be wrong, because the full hand was:

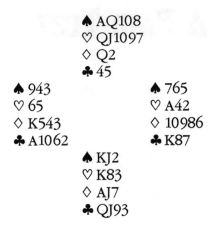

```
              ♠ AQ108
              ♡ QJ1097
              ◇ Q2
              ♣ 45
♠ 943                      ♠ 765
♡ 65                       ♡ A42
◇ K543                     ◇ 10986
♣ A1062                    ♣ K87
              ♠ KJ2
              ♡ K83
              ◇ AJ7
              ♣ QJ93
```

The Jack of clubs lost to the Ace and now there was no defense, because after a club return there would be a discard for dummy's diamond loser.

Kathie: A diamond back at trick two seems more natural and would certainly have been more effective.

Martin: The club would save a trick if South had something like KJx of diamonds and Ace of clubs, but it wouldn't beat the contract. East must ask himself, how can we make three tricks in the minor suits? And the answer is: only if we can take *two* tricks in clubs and one in diamonds.

Kathie: This brings up a rather tricky point. If East returns ◇ 10 at trick two and South lets it run, putting in the Jack, West may fail to lead a club. East's best play, therefore, is the ♣ K followed by a diamond, a real test for an expert defender.

52

A FAIR TEST

Dealer North Game all

```
          ♠ A
          ♡ J54
          ◊ KQ1098
          5
          ♣ K32
```

♠ 5 led

```
          ♠ KQ10
          ♡ A972
          ◊ 64
          ♣ A654
```

West	North	East	South
	1◊	pass	1♡
pass	2◊	pass	3NT
pass	pass	pass	

For many years each issue of the Bulletin of the International Bridge Press Association has carried four problems set by the former Swedish international, Jan Wohlin. The problems are sometimes easy, sometimes rather complicated. This is a good one because it's not so easy and the best play is very simple to describe.

West leads a spade, won by dummy's ace. What would you do next?

Would you cross to the Ace of clubs and lead a diamond to the 10? A small disaster follows when the full hand is like this:

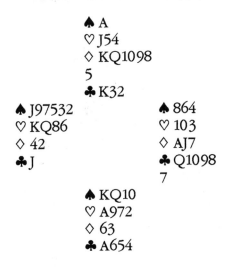

```
                    ♠ A
                    ♡ J54
                    ◊ KQ1098
                    5
                    ♣ K32
    ♠ J97532                    ♠ 864
    ♡ KQ86                      ♡ 103
    ◊ 42                        ◊ AJ7
    ♣ J                         ♣ Q1098
                               7
                    ♠ KQ10
                    ♡ A972
                    ◊ 63
                    ♣ A654
```

East wins with the Jack and forces out your remaining club stop. When he comes in with the ◊ A he cashes three more clubs. You have gone one down, losing two diamonds and three clubs.

Kathie: What a lovely hand! I'd like to think that instead of crossing to the ♣ A at trick two I would have led the ◊ 10 from dummy — not the Queen, of course.

Martin: Easy, you think? Put this hand into a club pairs and see how many declarers make the laydown ten tricks.

53

POINT THE WAY

Dealer South Game all

```
                      ♠ 76
                      ♡ 852
                      ◊ KQ103
                      ♣ AQ82
        ♠ 1054
        ♡ AKQ107
        6
        ◊ A2
        ♣ 73
```

West	North	East	South
			1♠
2♡	Dbl	pass	3♠
pass	4♠	pass	pass
pass			

North's double of 2♡ was negative. Against 4♠ West led the ♡ A, on which his partner dropped the Jack and declarer the 3. How should West plan the defense?

The deal was played in a pairs event and at several tables West followed with two more rounds of hearts. This did not embarrass the declarer because the full hand was:

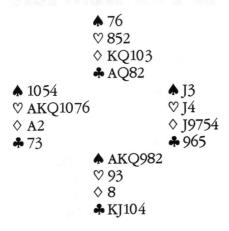

```
                    ♠ 76
                    ♡ 852
                    ◇ KQ103
                    ♣ AQ82
    ♠ 1054                      ♠ J3
    ♡ AKQ1076                   ♡ J4
    ◇ A2                        ◇ J9754
    ♣ 73                        ♣ 965
                    ♠ AKQ982
                    ♡ 93
                    ◇ 8
                    ♣ KJ104
```

East generally ruffed the third heart with the ♠ J, but South simply discarded his singleton diamond and made the rest of the tricks.

Kathie: I'm not very surprised at what happened. An experienced player in the West chair would have cashed the ◇ A at an early stage. Then the defenders can promote a trump trick. It's the only chance, really, in view of the bidding.

Martin: As a matter of fact, I was South at the table. The defense was accurate and my partner and I scored very poorly for going one down in four spades. As you say, it should be clear to West that the only chance for the defense is to take three top winners and make one trick in trumps. After the Ace of hearts, the perfect defense (nursing a moderate partner) is to cash ◇ A; then ♡ K, followed by a low heart to make absolutely sure that, if he holds a spade honor, partner will ruff.

54

ROOM FOR SUSPICION

Dealer East N-S vulnerable

```
                    ♠ A8654
                    ♡ K1032
                    ◊ Q7
                    ♣ K2
                              ♠ Q92
                              ♡ 876
            ◊ 4 led            ◊ A962
                              ♣ 743
```

West	North	East	South
		pass	1♣
pass	1♠	pass	2♣
pass	2♡	pass	2NT
pass	3NT	pass	pass
pass			

On West's lead dummy played the 7, East the Ace, and declarer the Jack. East returned the 2; now South produced the 3 and dummy's Queen won. The declarer forced out the ♣ A and finished with eleven tricks, losing just the two aces.

This was the full hand:

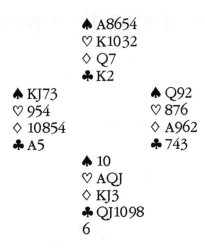

                    ♠ A8654
                    ♡ K1032
                    ◊ Q7
                    ♣ K2
    ♠ KJ73   ♠ Q92
    ♡ 954   ♡ 876
    ◊ 10854   ◊ A962
    ♣ A5   ♣ 743
                    ♠ 10
                    ♡ AQJ
                    ◊ KJ3
                    ♣ QJ1098
                    6

"We can save a trick or two if I switch to spades," East remarked. "But you might well have had five diamonds, the 3 was missing. I think I had to continue diamonds at trick two."

West seemed content with this analysis. But were the diamonds likely to be 2-2, and would a spade switch have been innocuous?

Kathie: The ◊ J was very likely a false card. With just a doubleton KJ in the unbid suit, South would probably have given preference to one of his partner's major suits.

Martin: That's true. And as for the other point, if East hopes to set up three tricks in spades he must lead the *Queen,* not a low one. It would be the same if he held K9x or J9x — he must lead the top card. There are several other situations of this sort, usually missed at the table.

Kathie: Going back to the first trick, I've an idea that the ◊ Q from dummy and the 3 from declarer's hand would have been more difficult for East to read.

THE ONLY CHANCE

organize the hand pattern better -- maybe even adjust the directions.

Dealer West Game all

```
            ♠ AKJ76
            ♡ QJ6
            ◊ A87
            ♣ K2
                      ♠ Q102
                      ♡ A3
            ♣ Q       ◊ 642
                      ♣ A10876
```

West	North	East	South
pass	1♠	pass	2♡
pass	4♡	pass	pass
pass			

When the ♣ Q held, West continued with a small club. East could see nothing better than to shift to a diamond.

116

This was the full deal:

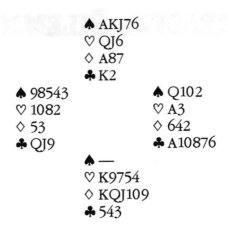

```
                    ♠ AKJ76
                    ♡ QJ6
                    ◇ A87
                    ♣ K2
   ♠ 98543                       ♠ Q102
   ♡ 1082                        ♡ A3
   ◇ 53                          ◇ 642
   ♣ QJ9                         ♣ A10876
                    ♠ —
                    ♡ K9754
                    ◇ KQJ109
                    ♣ 543
```

Declarer had no problem now in fulfilling his contract.

Kathie: I suppose it's not easy to see but a club continuation and hold-up of the first trump would promote partner's ten.

Martin: I don't think this would tax an expert defender. He would reflect that South responded 2♡ showing values. With only the ♡ K visible at this stage, declarer is marked with good diamonds.

Kathie: But, if declarer can read the defenders' intentions he may take countermeasures. After ruffing the third club in dummy, he will cash the ♠ AK, pitching two diamonds, and ruff a spade. When the Queen comes down, he plays a trump to the table. South must hold up, so declarer continues with the ♠ J, discarding another diamond. He now cashes two diamonds, finishing in dummy, and leads the fifth spade. The defense must surrender.

56

DREADFUL DILEMMA

Dealer South Game all

```
                    ♠ 92
                    ♡ 94
                    ◊ K
                    ♣ AKQJ8764
    ♠ 7543                      ♠ A1086
    ♡ KQ1073                    ♡ 652
    ◊ 10865                     ◊ J942
    ♣ —                        ♣ 109
                    ♠ KQJ
                    ♡ AJ8
                    ◊ AQ73
                    ♣ 532
```

West	North	East	South
			1NT
pass	6NT	pass	pass
pass			

North's 6NT was a sensible call. There might be two losers in one of the majors, but the suit would not necessarily be led.

West began with the ♡ K against 6NT and the declarer's first count revealed twelve top tricks — eight clubs, three diamonds and one heart. A confident claim might have worked against some opponents, but South rejected that stratagem because he could see that there might be an entry problem if the clubs were 2-0.

He won with ♡ A and played seven rounds of clubs to arrive at this position:

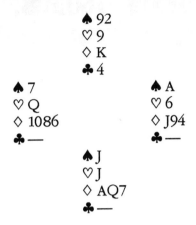

The lead of the last club caused many problems. East could see that if he parted with a heart, South would cash ◊K and throw him in with a spade. The best he could do was part with a diamond.

Now South dismissed the ♠ J and West—well, what do you want West to do? When a spade was thrown South cashed ◊K and exited with a heart.

Kathie: There's not much one can add to that little story. It shows what can be done when there is pressure in three suits.

Martin: One of the defenders said afterwards that it was like having a wife and two mistresses.

57

A DOOR CLOSES, ANOTHER DOOR OPENS

Dealer North N-S vulnerable

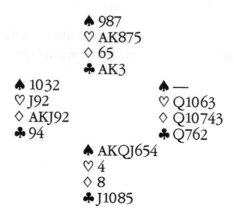

♠ 987
♡ AK875
◊ 65
♣ AK3

♠ 1032
♡ J92
◊ AKJ92
♣ 94

West	North	East	South
	1♡	pass	1♠
pass	2♣	pass	4♠
pass	5♠	pass	6♠
pass	pass	pass	

West led the ◊A, on which his partner played the 3 and declarer the 8. What should West play now? At the table West banged out another top diamond. This was not a success, because the full hand was:

♠ 987
♡ AK875
◊ 65
♣ AK3

♠ 1032   ♠ —
♡ J92   ♡ Q1063
◊ AKJ92   ◊ Q10743
♣ 94   ♣ Q762

♠ AKQJ654
♡ 4
◊ 8
♣ J1085

South ruffed the diamond at trick two, drew trumps, played the ♡ AK and ruffed a heart. When all followed, he was able to claim the contract.

Kathie: That was pretty dim of West, wasn't it? It was very clear from the bidding that South had diamond control. Also, if they were playing any kind of count system, East's 3 should have meant that he had an odd number, doubtless five. South is an entry short to establish the long heart if West plays a club at trick two.

Martin: West's argument at the time was that East would not have encouraged with 10xxx and that South might have held Qx, so it seemed best to rely on the diamonds. Do you show length or encouragement at this level? It is true that most good players like to have it both ways.

Kathie: Declarer can *still* succeed after the club shift on this hand. He wins the ♣K in dummy and plays six rounds of trumps. This is the end position:

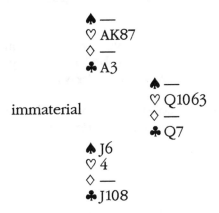

```
              ♠ —
              ♡ AK87
              ◊ —
              ♣ A3
                          ♠ —
                          ♡ Q1063
  immaterial               ◊ —
                          ♣ Q7
              ♠ J6
              ♡ 4
              ◊ —
              ♣ J108
```

On the next trump, dummy pitches a club and East is criss-cross trump squeezed. If the East-West heart holding were reversed, then a club shift at trick 2 would be fatal to the contract.

58

SECOND STRING

Dealer South Game all

       ♠ AQ3
       ♡ Q95
       ◇ J742
       ♣ K63

♠ 5 led

       ♠ KJ2
       ♡ AJ
       ◇ AK853
       ♣ AQ5

West	North	East	South
			2NT
pass	6NT	pass	pass
pass			

With 22 points and a five-card suit South was on the border of 2♣ in his system, to be followed by a non-forcing 2NT. He was content with a direct 2NT, however, and North had an obvious raise to 6NT.

West led a low spade and South, playing rather more quickly than usual, won in dummy and led the seven of diamonds.

He wasn't intending to run this, because if the diamonds were breaking well he wouldn't need the heart finesse, but it was possible that a defender holding Q1096 would cover the 7. Whether he thought about it or not (which would have been fatal), East played the 6, and on the King, West discarded a spade. South had no chance now, since the full hand was:

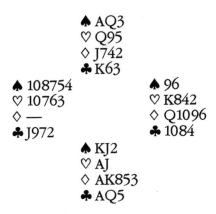

```
                    ♠ AQ3
                    ♡ Q95
                    ◊ J742
                    ♣ K63
     ♠ 108754                    ♠ 96
     ♡ 10763                     ♡ K842
     ◊ —                         ◊ Q1096
     ♣ J972                      ♣ 1084
                    ♠ KJ2
                    ♡ AJ
                    ◊ AK853
                    ♣ AQ5
```

"I could hardly make any safety play in diamonds," explained the declarer. "It would be silly to lose an unnecessary trick there and then have to take the heart finesse."

Kathie: There's something wrong with the reasoning there. Wouldn't it have been better to take the heart finesse first?

Martin: Yes, it would, though it's not so easy to see the point of that in time. If the heart finesse wins, then you make the safety play in diamonds

59

ONE OFF OR ONE OVER?

Dealer South Game all

         ♠ Q10
         ♡ 432
         ◇ 10976
         ♣ AKJ9

♡ 10 led

         ♠ A42
         ♡ A8765
         ◇ A
         ♣ 10854

West	North	East	South
			1♡
pass	2♣	pass	3♣
pass	3♡	pass	4♡
pass	pass	pass	

North-South promoted themselves into four hearts on this deal from rubber bridge, and West struck a trump lead. South let East hold the first trick with ♡ J and won the second. Then he led a low spade and put in dummy's 10. East won the Jack, drew a third round of trumps, and exited with the ♠ K. South had no way to dispose of his third spade, so he was one down.

```
                    ♠ Q10
                    ♡ 432
                    ◇ 10976
                    ♣ AKJ9
  ♠ 97653                        ♠ KJ8
  ♡ 109                          ♡ KQJ
  ◇ K8432                        ◇ QJ5
  ♣ Q                            ♣ 7632
                    ♠ A42
                    ♡ A8765
                    ◇ A
                    ♣ 10854
```

Everybody started talking at once.

"Thank you, partner," said East. "Your trump lead was vital."

"I put in dummy's ♠ 10, because if West had held the King he might have played it," explained the declarer. "But as East held both spade honors there was nothing I could do." Then North joined in to say that in his opinion the contract could have been made.

Kathie: North was right, wasn't he? South can play a sort of dummy reversal. After winning the second heart he cashes ◇ A, enters dummy three times in clubs and attempts to ruff three times. Then the ♠ A is his tenth trick.

Martin: And did you notice that if East discards on the fourth diamond instead of ruffing with ♡ K, he can be thrown in with it and be forced to lead a spade. That way, South makes an overtrick! This deal shows that you should consider which line offers the best chances when planning your play.

60

ONLY AN OVERTRICK

Dealer North E-W vulnerable

```
                    ♠ 84
                    ♡ 7632
                    ◊ AK5
                    ♣ KJ72

        ◊ Q led
                    ♠ J97
                    ♡ AQ10854
                    ◊ 4
                    ♣ AQ8
```

West	North	East	South
	pass	pass	1♡
pass	3♡	pass	4♡
pass	pass	pass	

West leads the Queen of diamonds. You win with the Ace in dummy, and East plays low. How do you set about the play?

Unfortunately you have no very valuable discard on the King of diamonds. If you lead a trump at trick two East will play the jack. A finesse loses to the King and West may have an awkward decision now, whether to attack spades or clubs. It's only a matter of an overtrick, but in some events overtricks are important.

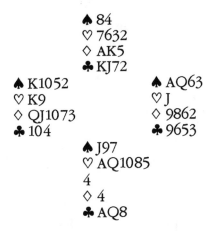

```
                    ♠ 84
                    ♡ 7632
                    ◇ AK5
                    ♣ KJ72
    ♠ K1052                   ♠ AQ63
    ♡ K9                      ♡ J
    ◇ QJ1073                  ◇ 9862
    ♣ 104                     ♣ 9653
                    ♠ J97
                    ♡ AQ1085
                    4
                    ◇ 4
                    ♣ AQ8
```

As you can see, a spade from West will give you a moderate result. You might have played differently, going up with the Ace of hearts and then playing on clubs, but this wouldn't work well because West would ruff the third club and by this time would know what to do. Do you see any better way to play the hand?

Kathie: It's not difficult with all the cards in view. You cash another diamond at trick two, discarding a club. Then when West comes in he will be tempted to lead a club, which will suit you very well.

Martin: There's one other small point. When you cash the second diamond East has the opportunity for a suit preference signal — the *nine* of diamonds. Then if South finesses in hearts, West will know that he must attack spades, not clubs.

61

IT DEPENDS

Dealer South Love all

```
              ♠ 10742
              ♡ 1084
              ◊ 4
              ♣ KQJ83
    ♠ 95
    ♡ AJ6
    ◊ A432
    ♣ A1052
```

West	North	East	South
			1♠
Dbl	3♠	4♡	4♠
Dbl	pass	pass	pass

West led the ♠ 5, and East's Queen was headed by the Ace. Without drawing a second round of trumps, South led the ♣ 7. It could hardly gain to hold up, so West went in with the ace, on which his partner dropped the 4.

What should West lead now, and why?

It is not so easy, because the ♠ 10 is probably an entry card, and then declarer's heart losers will go away on the clubs. After some thought West tried a low heart, and South made an overtrick.

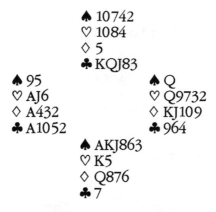

♠ 10742
♡ 1084
◊ 5
♣ KQJ83

♠ 95
♡ AJ6
◊ A432
♣ A1052

♠ Q
♡ Q9732
◊ KJ109
♣ 964

♠ AKJ863
♡ K5
◊ Q876
♣ 7

This happened in the final of a big team event and East wasn't pleased. "What do you think my four of clubs meant?" he demanded. "No point in giving you the count; I was telling you to try a low diamond."

Kathie: East made a fair point, but in a way I sympathize with West. With that club suit showing in dummy it's usual to give a length signal, isn't it?

Martin: Yes, but it's wrong to have any sort of rule about it. Here West couldn't possibly be interested in the number of clubs held by East — almost certainly three in any case. You will sometimes hear players say to one another, "Do you show length or strength with your signals?" The only answer to that is, it depends; normally length, but when this is not important, strength via suit preference.

62

UNFAIR COMMENT

Dealer East Love all

<pre>
                    ♠ AK84
                    ♡ A7632
                    ◊ 5
                    ♣ AJ8
        ♠ 106532
        ♡ 9
        ◊ AJ108743
        ♣ —
</pre>

West	North	East	South
		1NT	2♡
2♠	3♠	pass	3NT
5◊	5♡	pass	pass
Dbl	pass	pass	pass

Some of the bidding may look a bit odd when you see the full hand, but this is how it went in a 1958 world championship match between Italy and the USA. The Italians were East-West and East's 1NT was likely to be 15-16 or possibly 13-14 with a club suit. It was a natural part of the system for West to bid his weaker suit first.

The important question is what should West lead. Even with a 13-14 notrump opposite, 5♡ should be beatable, but partner is evidently minimum and almost certainly has values in diamonds rather than spades.

At any rate, Pietro Forquet began with the three of diamonds and the full hand was:

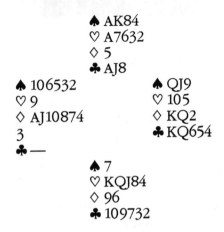

```
              ♠ AK84
              ♡ A7632
              ◊ 5
              ♣ AJ8
♠ 106532               ♠ QJ9
♡ 9                    ♡ 105
◊ AJ10874              ◊ KQ2
3                      ♣ KQ654
♣ —
              ♠ 7
              ♡ KQJ84
              ◊ 96
              ♣ 109732
```

East, Chiaradia, won the diamond lead and returned a low club, for West to ruff. There was still a club trick to come.

Kathie: I remember this hand, of course — was it over 35 years ago? It created a sensation for a number of reasons. Today the underlead from the strong diamonds would scarcely raise an eyebrow.

Martin: Quite so, but a player like Forquet was ahead of his time. I was hardly in the tournament world myself in those days, but I read about this deal later. The editor of the Bridge World at the time, Sonny Moyse Jr., wrote: "The charge of cheating levelled against certain members of the Italian team was based as much on this deal as on any other." Unfair, don't you think?

63

SAFE COVER

Dealer East Love all

```
                    ♠ A73
                    ♡ 985
                    ◊ 87
                    ♣ KQJ109
        ♠ 10965               ♠ QJ82
        ♡ 7                   ♡ KJ64
        ◊ J9532               ◊ 1064
        ♣ 654                 ♣ 83
                    ♠ K4
                    ♡ AQ1032
                    ◊ AKQ
                    ♣ A72
```

West	North	East	South
		pass	2♣
pass	3♣	pass	3♡
pass	4♡ (1)	pass	4NT
pass	5◊	pass	7♡ (2)
pass	pass	pass	

(1) This was an underbid, really; most modern players
    would temporize with three spades.
(2) And this was an overbid by any reckoning.

It is unusual to make the four of trumps by force when
defending against a grand slam. I happened on this deal
from a tournament in Bermuda.

East, the Bermudian international David Ezekiel, had kept very quiet with his KJ64 in the trump suit and may not have been very pleased at first when his partner led the seven of hearts. Dummy's 8 was covered by the Jack and Queen, and later the 9 by the King and Ace. A trick or two later the position was:

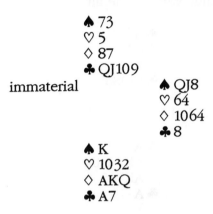

♠ 73
♡ 5
◊ 87
♣ QJ109

immaterial

♠ QJ8
♡ 64
◊ 1064
♣ 8

♠ K
♡ 1032
◊ AKQ
♣ A7

When the 5 of hearts was led from dummy East did not omit to cover with the 6.

Kathie: The lead didn't matter, as it happened, But did you notice that when the 8 of hearts is led East mustn't fail to cover?

Martin: It would be an awkward decision at trick two. If South held six hearts the cover would be a mistake.

ONE TO KEEP

Dealer West Game all

♠ K864
♡ 62
◇ 532
♣ KQ86

♣ 10 led

♠ A
♡ AKQJ104
◇ AK765
♣ A

West	North	East	South
pass	pass	pass	2♣
pass	2◇	pass	2♡
pass	3♣	pass	3◇
pass	3NT	pass	5♡
pass	6♡	pass	pass
pass			

There was a time when many North players would have made a positive response on the fair values, but positive responses tend to lose time and it is common these days to begin quite useful hands with a negative.

West began with the ♣ 10 and South could see nothing better than to play off six rounds of trumps, ♠ A, and then a *low* diamond.

This would have been brilliant play if either defender had retained a singleton Queen of diamonds (or had allowed his partner to win with a singleton jack). It didn't quite work on this occasion because the full hand was:

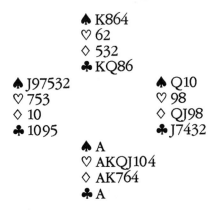

♠ K864
♡ 62
◇ 532
♣ KQ86

♠ J97532   ♠ Q10
♡ 753   ♡ 98
◇ 10   ◇ QJ98
♣ 1095   ♣ J7432

♠ A
♡ AKQJ104
◇ AK764
♣ A

East kept four diamonds among his last five cards and was able to exit with a diamond, forcing the declarer to lose a second trick.

Kathie: I don't suppose I would have seen it at the table, but I know that a clever play was possible on this hand. South cashes the Ace of spades and just two rounds of hearts, followed by the ◇AK. If the diamonds break 4-1, he exits with the 4 of hearts and West has to give dummy the lead.

Martin: Unless, of course, West has been clever enough to retain the 3 of hearts!